THE CALL TO SERVICE

THE CALL TO SERVICE

A Sermon Series

By

Clinton L. Ryan, Th.D., Litt., FRSA

Minister of the Oughton Road Church
New Testament Church of God
11-13 Oughton Road, Highgate, Birmingham B12 0DF

and

Programme Coordinator
Canada Christian College
&
School of Graduate Theological Studies

The Call to Service

First edition 2013

Rev. Dr. Clinton L. Ryan

Birmingham, UK

Copyright © 2013 Clinton L. Ryan

Edited, designed and published by Capital Cube Creatives

Birmingham, UK

ISBN 978-1-905028-56-6

All scripture is taken from the King James Version of the Bible unless otherwise stated.

Dedication

Dedicated to the members and friends
of the Oughton Road church.

The ministers, members and friends
of the Highgate District.

The many students who have studied
with me.

CONTENTS

FOREWORD

The contents of this book are listed among some of the last sermons that I delivered as Minister of the Oughton Road Church, Birmingham, before I retired from Pastoral Ministry of the local church and District Minister of the Highgate group of churches.

It has been a great priviledge to serve the local congregation, the congregations on the District and the community, also the students who have studied within this Collegiate church from home and abroad. We have had a blessed pilgrimage together.

My reason for delivering these sermons was to remind the members of the churches, graduates and students of Abraham's confidence in the faithfulness of God. It was also to remind them that Abraham was not ashamed to build an altar to God and to worship Him in the presence of the heathen.

By doing so he declared his expectation of the fulfilment of the Divine promise. Properly understood his actions serve as antecedents for Christians today. We can venture forth in faith and confidence in the promises of God. To respond positively to the command of God is the greatest service that any man or woman can do.

Clinton L Ryan

THE CALL TO SERVICE

Now the LORD had said unto Abram, Get thee out of thy country, and from thy kindred, and from thy father's house, unto a land that I will show thee.
Gen. 12:1

There is absolutely no doubt, that the cost of obedience is small when compared to the cost of disobedience and its consequences. Supporting evidence for this is to be found repeatedly in Scripture, in personal experience and history. It is a truism of the Christian faith that the call of God to Abraham was wrapped in a package.

The call of God has never come without a commission, opportunity, promise, responsibility, sacrifice and a command to separation; an adventure to pilgrimage and it is always permanent. These are some of the things that we have learnt from studying the lives of God's servants who have ministered prior to us and those who faithfully minister among us.

When the LORD called Abram, He said unto him [Gen. 12:1-2] "...Get thee out of thy country, and from thy kindred, and from thy father's house, unto a land that I will show thee: And I will make of thee a great nation, and I will bless thee, and make thy name great; and thou shalt be a blessing." An unknown author has described the call of God and the response of man as the greatest of commitments.

To accept as fact what this author has said: is to acknowledge that commitment has a number of emphasises:

1. It is reciprocal in function
2. It is vertical in connection
3. It is horizontal in relationship
4. It is practical in delivery
5. It is contagious in outreach
6. It is identifiable in reflection

The person, who makes a wholehearted response to the call of God, will be ready and willing to make the ultimate sacrifice in service and in worship. The sacrifice that, that person will make, can be described as the difference between involvement and commitment, this can be seen as an "Egg and ham breakfast." The reality is that the hen was involved, but the pig was committed.

The call of God is not simply about involvement, it is about absolute commitment. It is miraculous and mysterious that the Creator of mankind made it His primary function to call people into His service. That He called ordinary men and women and entrusted them with an extraordinary work to do.

In his appeal, observation and testimony to live in absolute commitment to the call of God, William Cowper wrote:

> *O for a closer walk with God, A calm and heavenly frame;*
> *A light to shine upon the road That leads me to the Lamb.*
> *The dearest idol that I know What e'er that idol be, Help*
> *me to tear it from Thy throne And worship only Thee.*

There are three things for our consideration as we examine the "Call of God to Abraham:"[1]

Excellence in the Calling
Antecedent in the Calling
Understanding the Primary Call

Excellence in the Calling:

God did not call him to serve with mediocrity; He called him to serve with excellence. The service in which we are engaged is primarily a service of selfless-excellence; it is a demanding and practical service. Thus, we do the work as the servants of God. It is important also to know that a person does not have to be qualified when God calls him or her. He often calls people who are willing and then qualifies them.

Elizabeth Dole, sought to remind us of some biblical and practical ideals when she wrote about our "High and holy Calling." Those of us who are privileged to own a copy or, copies of the Bible and some of us have many copies and

---

1   Gen. 6:8; 12:1-2; Ex. 2:5-10; 3:1-22; Josh. 1:1-7; Jer. 1:1-5; Isa. 6:1-10

different versions in the quest for simplicity and clarity.

It is not simply what we are called by God to do that matters, but what the sovereign God calls us and chooses us by His grace and mercy to do. What is absolutely certain is, He has not called us to worldly success, but to faithfulness and obedience. He has called us to bring the whole of our lives in submission to His will in the plan of world redemption.

If this call of God is understood in the revelation of Holy Scripture, then we know that life is not just a few years to spend on self-indulgence and career development and advancement. But it is a privilege, an opportunity, a responsibility and a stewardship to be lived according to a much higher calling. It is this that gives true and permanent meaning to life.

In his encouragement to people to be effective and committed in their calling, both sacred and secular, Martin Luther King, Jr. said, "If a man is called to be a street-sweeper, he should sweep streets even as Michelangelo painted, or Beethoven played music, or Shakespeare wrote poetry. He should sweep streets so well that all the hosts of heaven and earth will pause to say, here lived a great street-sweeper who did his job well."[2]

---

2   Ex. 12:1-14; Isa 53:1-2; John 1:29-31

Antecedent in the Calling:

What lessons can we learn from the call of God to Abraham? From he responded to the call of God, he became a pilgrim. His experiences in life can be likened to the course of a long river that had meandered its way through difficult territories, such as Ur of the Chaldeans, Egypt and Palestine. But always he was moving by faith, believing the promises of God.

Like the course of the river, with its many windings, its ebbs and flows, it seemed to have given depth and became stronger as it made its way to its destination. Abram's experiences were deepened, his name changed and he developed in strength as he followed the guidance of the LORD. He alone in all of scripture was called the friend of God. [James 2:23] "... The scripture was fulfilled which saith, Abraham believed God, and it was imputed unto him for righteousness and he was called the friend of God."

The Greek word that James used and we have translated friend is 'philos', but this does not simply describe the friendship between two human beings. This was a friendship between the uncreated God and created man. It was a unique relationship between the immortal and the mortal. It was the closest and most pleasant relationship that any man could have had with God.

It was a covenantal relationship sealed with the blood

of circumcision and absolute commitment in service. That commitment was undivided and unreserved as he travelled with his son Isaac to the place of sacrifice on mount Moriah. On this most fateful of journeys, when Isaac asked [22:7-8] "...My father: and he answered, here am I my son. And he said, Behold the fire and the wood: but where is the lamb for a burnt offering?"

God did not tell Abraham what the result of his obedience would be – That would be like giving the result of an examination before the questions were read. But Abraham held steadfastly to his faith in his covenant relationship and obedience to God. The miracles and mysteries of God always function in the realms of blessings for those whom God calls.[3]

When Abraham had reached that crucial place of sacrificing his son, the covenant keeping and covenant making God intervened [Gen 22:10-12] "...Abraham stretched forth his hand, and took the knife to slay his son. And the angel of the LORD called unto him out of heaven, and said, Abraham, Abraham: and he said, here am I. And he said, Lay not thine hand upon the lad, neither do thou anything unto him: for now I know that thou fearest God, seeing that thou hast not withheld thy son, thine only son from me."

---

3   C. L. Ryan, Understanding the Ministerial Call, Birmingham: Oughton Road Church Ministries, 2003

This level of commitment is not recorded anywhere else in scripture, but it reveals a pre-view of the commitment of God to make the ultimate sacrifice to redeem mankind. In his understanding of God's determination to redeem the lost souls of mankind, John said [John 3:16] "For God so loved the world, that he gave his only begotten Son, that whosoever believeth in him should not perish but have everlasting life." The life of faith that Abraham lived will always be fragrant with the blessings of God, and not only Abraham, but also all those who accept the call of God and the package that comes with it.

Understanding the Primacy of the Call:

To understand the primacy of the call of God upon Abraham's life, we have to follow the course of the Abrahamic experiences as we would follow the course of a winding river. To do so will help us to understand more clearly God's call to service and worship. In our quest for information, we can ask a number of basic questions:

When Did God Call Him?
How Did God Call Him?
What Command God Gave Him?
How Was His Life Changed?
God Continues To Call.

When Did God Call Him?

God called him while he lived in the land of Chaldea

[Gen. 11:31]; he was living in idolatry and ignorance. The apostle Paul opened the curtains of ancient history to give us a glimpse of what was happening when he heard the call of God and how he responded to the call and what was contained in the package.

The following is part of what he wrote [Rom. 4:c8-13]

> *"...Blessed is the man to whom the Lord will not impute sin. Cometh this blessedness then upon the circumcision[4] only, or upon the un-circumcision also? For we say, that faith was reckoned to Abraham for righteousness. How was it then reckoned? When he was in circumcision or un-circumcision? Not in circumcision, but in un-circumcision. And he received the sign of circumcision, a seal of the righteousness of faith which he had yet being uncircumcised: that he might be the father of all them that believe, though they be not circumcised; that the righteousness might be imputed unto them also.*
> *And the father of circumcision to them who are not of the circumcision only, but who also walk in the steps of that faith of our father Abraham, which he had being yet uncircumcised. For the promise, that he should be the heir*

---

4 Circumcision was a sign of separation, the blood that was the seal of Covenant relationship between God and the individual and the community – the community of Israel.

Baptism is an outward sign of an inward work of Grace. It is a public testimony of repentance from sin by an individual to become a member of the Church – the community of the Redeemed.

of the world, was not to Abraham or his seed, through the law, but through the righteousness of faith."

Abraham was not called because he was more righteous than his fellow countrymen. The God that made and kept covenants did not seek for someone that was righteous or worthy. He called someone that He knew who would follow Him in faithfulness and absolute obedience, not counting the cost of what he would leave behind.

The apostle Paul assured the saints in Rome, that the call of God was extended to sinful mankind. God appealed to them to repent and renounce sin and be made righteous. This is what he said, [Rom. 5:8] "But God commendeth his love towards us, in that while we were yet sinners, Christ died for us." It was the blood of Jesus Christ that atoned for Abraham, when he heard the call of God and responded gladly and willingly.

How did God call him?

The scripture has not given us the method that God employed in calling Abraham. Whether he heard an audible voice, a messenger was sent to him, or the Holy Spirit revealed the call in his heart. Without interviewing Abraham, we will never know; what we know is that the call was arresting, compelling and personal, it was so awesome that he could not resist it.

In the calling of God to Abraham, two distinct things are

revealed [1] the privilege to serve and [2] the responsibility to serve. I am conscious that I am being repetitive, but I want you as a theological student to know that, the call of God to this sacred ministry is the greatest privilege an individual can be given and it comes with the greatest of individual responsibilities.

God did not call Abraham so that he could be better than his neighbours, or that he could be better than any member of his family. God called him that He could make him a better person than he was and to make him, His elected servant and the Father of the people of circumcision. God chooses men and women for special occasions and situations. What has He chosen you to be and do?

The men and women that God chooses and who answer the call to serve can be likened to a pen in the hand of a writing God, who is sending love letters to individuals and to a world in need. In the gospel accounts, when Jesus called His disciples, He made it clear that the calling, choosing and privilege was all His. [John 15:16] "...Ye have not chosen me, but I have chosen you, and ordained you, that ye should go and bring forth fruit, and that your fruit should remain: that whatsoever ye shall ask of the Father in my name, he may give it you."

An unknown author has left us with this observation, "God doesn't ask about your ability, only your availability; and, if you prove your dependability, the Lord will increase your capability." The story was told of a woman visiting a clinic, she saw a nurse attending the sores of a leprosy patient. "I would not do that for a million pounds." She remarked, the nurse answered, "Neither would I, But I do it for Jesus for nothing." We may never be certain by what method God and His Son, call individuals, but here are the terms and conditions that Jesus laid down in the gospel.

This is applicable and relevant to every person who answers the call of God for world redemption [Matt. 16:24-25] "... Jesus said unto his disciples, If any man will come after me, let him deny himself, and take up his cross and follow me. For whosoever will save his life shall lose it: and whosoever will lose his life for my sake shall find it." Mother Teresa, wrote: "Let us touch the dying, the poor and the lonely and the unwanted according to the graces we have received and let us not be ashamed or slow to do the humble work."

What Command did God give him?

God commanded him to live a life of sanctification. The command was for him to separate himself from the life-style of idolatry. When the command of God was heard, it seemed to have had embraced the thought, you cannot any more cope with your private plans, or the place of your family dwelling. I am calling you to a world-changing destiny, to the headship of the covenant people.[5]

---

5 Ex. 20:1-17; 2 Cor. 6:11-18; Rom. 1:17-32

The sovereign command said [Gen. 12:3] "... I will bless them that bless thee, and curse him that curseth thee: and in thee shall all the families of the earth be blessed." Some modern leaders do not believe in absolutes, they believe that all things are relative. But the command was that nothing, absolutely nothing should hinder him from serving and worshipping God faithfully and devotedly. Not country, not family and certainly not the life-style of his father's house. He had to break with the religion of polytheism and cling to monotheism.

The "Sinai Commandments" were not yet given, but Abraham must have had a preview of the following: "Thou shalt not have any other gods before me. Thou shalt not make unto thee any graven image...Thou shalt not bow down thyself to them, nor serve them... Thou shalt not take the name of the LORD thy God in vain..." Every association, connection, friendship and relationship that came between Abraham and the call of God had to be disconnected and left behind.

The command was a summons to sacrificial living. When a man is so called of God, any action done to cling to God in communion of holiness is a true sacrifice. An absolute surrender to the sovereignty of God. If a man is not ready and willing to disconnect from his past, Paul called the past, the "old things" [2 Cor. 5:17] "Old things are passed away." He cannot truly answer the call of God, as was required of Abraham. No sacrifice can be too great to make for Him, who gave his life for us.

The man, or woman who answers the "Divine call," has a new life of faith in God and fellowship with the "Holy Trinity." This is called the "Blessed life." It is the transformed life of which we read in Pauline theology [Rom. 12:2] "...And be not conformed to this world: but be ye transformed by the renewing of your mind, that ye may prove what is that good, and acceptable, and perfect, will of God." It is the transplanting by the Holy Spirit from the barren soil of self into the fruitful and fertile soil of divine grace.

What Possession did God Promise?

The LORD promised Abraham a "land that he would show him: for a possession." Many people hesitate when God calls them to the life of faith. They contemplate what they have to give up and what they will have to leave behind. Some seek advisers who tell them: you can give an egg, but to give the bacon is too much. When God called Abraham, He urged him to disconnect from the material, political, religious and social possessions that he had, and that he had known all his life and had grown accustomed to. God had already prepared new possessions for him.[6]

---

6   Ex. 9:27 Pharoah made an honest confession in which he acknowledged his arrogance.

Luke 15:18 The Prodigal son used the same words for his confession – 'I have sinned'

God is no man's debtor. In Luke's gospel, Jesus told a story about a father and his two sons. The tradition of inheritance of the time afforded the youngest son of this family to make an unjust demand upon his father's estate [Luke 15:11-32], the key verses that I am about to use read [21-24] "...Father, I have sinned against heaven, and in thy sight, and am no more worthy to be called thy son. But the father said to his servant, Bring forth the best robe, and put it on him; and put a ring on his hand, and shoes on his feet: and bring hither the fatted calf, and kill it; and let us eat and be merry: for this my son was dead, and is alive again; he was lost, and is found..."

It is very obvious that he had to leave the pigs and the pigs sty and begin the journey home. He had to give up the rags and be washed and made clean and he had to give up the old broken sandals, before he could put on the new robe, the new shoes, he had to receive the ring of family reconciliation, before he could sit and eat at the family table. This father had prepared in faith for his son's coming home. One of the hardest things in life is to become disconnected from the past. The past can be the robber of the future.

The apostle Paul took this view when he wrote [2 Cor. 5:17-18] "Therefore if any man be in Christ, he is a new creature: old things are passed away; behold all things are become new. And all things are of God, who hath reconciled us unto himself by Jesus Christ, and hath given to us the ministry of reconciliation." Yes! When a man comes into vital union with Jesus Christ, old things are passed away, he becomes disconnected from them.

Abraham's possessions also embraced a number of blessings. The first is that God promised to bless him personally, second, God promised to make him a blessing, third, God promised to make his name great, fourth, God promised to bless those who would blessed him, fifth, God promised to bless all the families of the earth through him; this means through the "Greater Abraham" – Jesus Christ. This is how Judeo–Christian theology is understood.[7]

All of these things were promised to Abraham and they were fulfilled as he obeyed and followed the leading of the LORD. Wealth and worldly wisdom will not gain for us eternal life. There is no blessing and everlasting peace for those who reject the call of God and stop short of accepting Jesus Christ as Saviour, no matter what they achieve in this life. Not far from the kingdom, is still outside of the kingdom. Almost means to be lost.

God continues to call:

God, however, still extends the call to service and worship; one of the grand old hymns of the Christian faith says:

> *It may not be on the mountain's height, Or over the stormy*

---

7 Ps. 4:5; Prov. 10:2; Isa. 58:8; Rom. 4:6; Heb. 11:7; Jam. 3:18

sea, It may not be at the battle's front, My lord will have need of me, But if by a still small voice, He calls, To the path that I do not know. I'll answer, dear Lord, with my hand in Thine, I'll go where you want me to go.

Perhaps today there are loving words, Which Jesus would have me speak; There may be now in the paths of sin, Some wand'rer whom I should seek; O Saviour if Thou wilt be my guide, Though dark and rugged the way, My voice shall echo the message sweet, I'll say what You want me to say.

This hymn sums-up well the response of Abraham to God's call and commission. Would you respond to God's call in the same way? Would you partner with God in world redemption?

THE SOJOURN IN HARAN

Abram departed, as the LORD had spoken unto him;
and Lot went with him: and Abram was seventy and
five years old when he departed out of Haran.
Gen. 12:4

The picture we draw from this text is that Abraham was led by Terah his father rather than the direct command of God. The command of God was, "...unto a land that I will show thee." Under Terah's leadership, Abram pitched his tent in Haran. This raises some serious questions that you and I have to ask one another:[1]

Have you pitched your tent when God has commanded you to be on the move?
Have you pitched your tent in Haran when Gods command is to journey on, until He shows you where He wants you to be?
Have you pitched your tent in the land of spiritual,

---

1 Gen. 4:20; 7:8; Ps. 15:1; Acts 18:3

Babylon, the capital of Babylonia, laid on both sides of the Euphrates. Here was the beginning of the kingdom of Nimrod (Gen. 10:10), and here the tower of Babel was erected. Historically, this city was important until about 1830 B.C. when its first dynasty was established. The city reached its greatest heights in the reigns of Hammurabi (1800 B.C.) and Nebuchadnezzar (605-562 B.C.) who conquered Judah and carried the Jews into captivity.

intellectual and material famine where God has drawn double yellow lines?

Have you pitched your tent where the enemy can hide the Babylonian garment within?

Have you pitched your tent where the insurgent can make you a target?

Have you pitched your tent where a kinsfolk's voice can speak negatively in your ears? .

Have you pitched your tent outside of the purpose and will of God?

Haran was a business city through the centre of which ran the main highway that linked the Mediterranean course to the Euphrates River. It was the stronghold of the Babylonian Moon Cult. The city of Haran was founded by some Samarian people from Ur of Chaldea; it is believed that some of them were kinsfolk of Terah. It was not until after the death of Terah that Abraham obeyed the command of God.

Two Kinds of Wisdom:

It is safe to say two kinds of wisdom were in opposition here.

[1] Divine wisdom and
[2] Worldly wisdom

The latter is inadequate in the life of faith. There is no resting place or, blessing for those who disobey the command of God and His Son Jesus Christ. It does not matter how far people have travelled or, how many years they have served. The command was not to pitch our tents where worldly wisdom demands or decides.

Terah only sought his own comfort when he commanded Abraham to abort his pilgrimage and dwell in Haran. Is there someone who is telling you to abort your pilgrimage and pitch your tent in Haran? Are they telling you about an event, when God has spoken to you about a process? The LORD'S destination for Abram was Canaan, the "Land of Promise," but it could never be possessed in the spirit of worldly wisdom. God had designed a process for the fulfilment of His promise.

There must be the experience of crossing the river Euphrates; this was to serve as a type of baptism. There had to be a type of public demonstration of the passing of the old way of life to the beginning of entering into the new life. He had to go through the desert successfully if he was to enjoy the blessings of Canaan.[2]

Today's Christians need to learn from Scripture that those who have broken God's heart are those who have obeyed

---

2 Nearly every individual and group that God has delivered has experienced some form of baptism. Israel in the Red Sea (Ex. 14:21-22; 1 Cor. 10:1-4) Jacob's crossing of the river (Gen. 31:21) was a symbol of baptism; he was on his way to be reconciled to his brother. In both cases baptism speaks of a fresh start and a new beginning.

half of God's commandment and disobeyed the other half. Believers who abide on the border of faith, or sit on the fence half committed cannot inherit the fullness of the promise of God. The ancient historian reminds us of the promise of God to another leader [Josh. 1:3] "... Every place that the sole of your foot shall tread upon, that I have given unto you, as I said unto Moses."

A Purposeful Journey

The journey of faith is always forward and upward. Many of the great hymn writers have affirmed this. In his affirmation, Johnson Oatman, wrote:

> I'm pressing on the upward way, New heights I'm gaining everyday - Still praying as I'm onward bound, Lord plant my feet on higher ground.
>
> My heart has no desire to stay, Where doubts arise, and fears dismay; Though some may dwell where these abound, My constant aim is higher ground.
>
> Beyond the mist I fain would rise, to rest beneath the unclouded skies, Above earth's turmoil peace is found, By those who dwell on higher ground.
>
> I long to scale the utmost height, Though rough the way, and hard the fight, My song while climbing, shall resound, Lord, lead me on to higher ground.
>
> Lord, lead me up the mountain side, I dare climb without my Guide; And heaven gained, I'll gaze

around, With grateful heart from higher ground.

In the fifth verse of our context we read, "They went forth to go into the land of Canaan: and into the land of Canaan they came." Are some of the most purposeful and precious words of obedience in the calling of any man's life. Added to this, we read in verse nine "...Going on still toward the south." The question can be asked, what did Abram and the people go out from? They went out from a life of idolatry, poverty, failure, sin, maliciousness, hatred, hopelessness, helplessness, purposelessness and worldly pleasures.[3]

What Kind of Place was Haran?

What was offered in exchange? The covenant and unfailing promises of God. No longer did they have to lean on their own feelings, human wisdom and understanding. The advice of Solomon is so appropriate here [Prov. 3:5] "Trust in the LORD with all thine heart and lean not unto thine own understanding." Abram began the journey as the Scripture say, "He went out not knowing whither he went." This was a divinely planned journey – a journey of faith.

If Abram knew William Williams' great hymn, he would

---

3   The successful pilgrim must begin his or her journey in the name of our God; but must also be sure to have with him or her two important things (1) humility (2) charity.

have sung:

> *Guide me, O Thou Great Jehovah! Pilgrim through this barren land; I am, but thou art mighty. Hold me with Thy powerful hand: Bread of heaven! Feed me now and evermore."*

> *Open Thou the crystal fountain, Whence the healing stream doth flow; Let the fiery, cloudy pillar, Lead me all my journey through: Strong Deliverer! Be Thou still my strength and shield.*

The pilgrimage had to pass through difficult territory. The historian wrote [v.6] "Abraham passed through the land unto the place of Sichem, unto the plain of Moreh. And the Canaanite was in the land." This journey went through the Syrian Desert and Abraham was to encounter some of the nations that the Bible described as evildoers or heathen.

The Deuteronomic historian wrote [7:1] "When the LORD God shall bring thee into the land whither thou goest to possess it, and hath cast out many nations before thee, the Hittites, and the Girgashites, and the AMORITES, and the Canaanites, and the Perizzites, and the Hivites, and the Jebusites, seven nations greater and mightier than thou." Not only was the journey a difficult one, but also the people they would meet would be difficult as we read.[4]

---

4 Isaiah 43:1-7

There is no doubt that the passage into blessing and glory was extremely testing to the flesh, blood and bones. It was so with Jesus Christ. The way to the Promised Land was full of sorrow, the enemies of Abram jeered and mocked him and his brethren along the way, but he had not yet reached the end of the journey. The lesson we can learn from here is that when Jesus Christ went to the cross all the burden and sins of common humanity were laid on Him.

He opened the entrance into the fullness of the blessings and forgiveness for each person and for every person through the barren desert of catastrophe and heathenism.

The Entrance:

The entrance into Canaan is revealed in the victorious phrase [v.5],"...into the land of Canaan they came." Abraham came out of the Chaldea in obedience and now he had entered Canaan in obedience. Whatever God begins, He will bring to a successful conclusion. There is another lesson to be learnt from the entrance into Canaan and that is: those who go out in obedience and expectation of faith will not be left in the confusion and desert of disappointment.

We also learn that there are two common and major reasons for failure in the Christian life. [1] Is stopping short of where God stands, it holds up the purpose and promise for the individual and the church, and [2] going with the divine command and promise. To go in the energy of the flesh is to fail; it is to have no special direction from God to be guided by. Thus as the parable says: "In the heat of sunny-temptation they wither and die spiritually, having no root. They cannot draw on any spiritual resource.

The Psalmist reminds us that the man who makes obedience to God his delight [Ps. 1:3] "... Shall be like the tree planted by the rivers of water, that bringeth forth his fruit in his season; his leaf also shall not wither; and whatsoever he doeth shall prosper." Our entrance into the blessings of God is linked to our obedience to His call and commandment. Abraham was called out of Chaldea that he might enter into Canaan. Christians too are called out – that we may enter into the fullness of the promise of God.

Inescapable Experiences:

The last phrase of verse six says, "...The Canaanite was in the land," is a sobering reminder that Abram and his family were on a pilgrimage and that they were living in the real world. Their enemies were many and everywhere. With this sobering thought, I have to disagree with William M. Golden, in his great hymn "Where the Soul Never Dies."

The land of Canaan cannot be a type of heaven, since Scripture repeatedly declare heaven to be a place without enemies and sinful practices. This is confirmed by the "Ten Commandments", "The Covenant at Horeb" and

"The Great Commandments."

The LORD affirmed this through the lips of the prophet Micah saying [Mic. 6:8] "He hath showed thee O man, what is good; and what doth the LORD require of thee, but to do justly, and to love mercy, and to walk humbly with thy God? This is also affirmed by the call to repentance in the books of the prophets of Israel, the Gospels and the Epistles.

There are also many hymn writers who have written about the purity of and sin-less-ness of heaven. In his hymn "Sin Can Never Enter There." C.W. Naylor wrote

Heaven is a holy place, filled with glory and with grace, Sin can never enter there; All within its gates are pure. From defilement kept secure, Sin can never enter there.

If you hope to dwell at last, When your life on earth is past, In that home so bright and fair, You must here be cleansed from sin, Have the life of Christ within, Sin can never enter there.

The reality of the Land of Canaan is symbolic of the new relationship into which Abram and those who travelled with him had entered after obeying and trusting in God and had gone forth in His guidance, command and promise. The Lord had said to Abram "Get thee out of thy country... unto a land that I will show thee." Abraham's father Terah had made a private plan, but the LORD had revealed a world –affecting destiny.[5]

The Land of Canaan that we sing about as Christians is typical of the new relationships into which we have come by trusting God and journeying on in the name of Jesus Christ or Saviour. In this world, we will have tribulation and warfare and as pilgrims and strangers, we will have need of continual faith support. Being in the place of trials and warfare, we are in the place where God promised to bless. Abram was not specially blessed while he was in his comfort zone.

It was his obedience to God's command and stepping out in faith that he and those who were with him were blessed. They experienced the enmity and hostility of seven nations, but God brought them through to the Promise Land – the Jerusalem of which they sang. The battles that they faced were not theirs but the LORD'S.

To us modern Christians the hymn writer George Duffield says:

> Stand up! Stand up for Jesus, The trumpet call obey; Forth to the mighty conflict, In this His glorious day; Ye that are men now serve Him, Against unnumbered foes; Let courage rise with danger, And strength to strength oppose."

When the Christians in Ephesus were faced with similar problems, the apostle Paul cautioned [Eph. 6:11] "Put on

---

5   Rom. 8:28-39; Heb. 11:1-40

the whole armour of God that ye may be able to stand against the wiles of the devil..." The American country singer Dolly Parton said "The way I see it, if you want the rainbow, you gotta put up with the rain."

The Guaranteed Assurance:

The LORD said to Abram [v.7] "Unto thy seed will I give this land, this was followed by the building of an altar for sacrifice and worship. The fullness of the promise was experienced when Abram and his people went into the land. When by faith the Christians take their stand on the promises of God's words, they will find sweet fulfilment in their experiences.

This was what Fanny J. Crosby, wrote about in her hymn,

> Blessed assurance – Jesus is mine! Oh, what a foretaste of glory divine, Heir of salvation, purchase of God; Born of His Spirit, washed in His blood.

She structured the verses so beautifully for us, when she placed the centre of God's promises in Jesus Christ. We shall pitch our tents in Haran, if we partly obey God's command.

The apostle Paul encouraged the saints in Corinth to go all the way to obtain the fullness of the promises of God [2 Cor. 1:20] "All the promises of God in him [Jesus Christ] are yea and in him amen, unto the glory of God by us." As Abram went forth with those who shared his journey, so can the Christians – you and I, into the heart and centre of all God's promises and purposes in Jesus Christ.

We will find grace sufficient there. The anxious soul must get to the centre before the full assurance of salvation is received. The apostle recorded these words of Jesus [Matt. 10:22] "He that endureth to the end shall be saved." Paul also encouraged the Christians in Ephesus to maintain their trust in God and continue to the end of the journey [Eph. 1:13-14] "In whom ye also trusted, after that ye have the word of truth, the gospel of your salvation: in whom also after that ye believed, ye were sealed with that Holy Spirit of promise, Which is the earnest of our inheritance until the redemption of the purchased possession, unto the praise of his glory."

THE TENT AND THE ALTAR

He removed from thence unto a mountain on the east of Bethel, and pitched his tent, having Bethel on the west, and Hai on the east: and there he builded an altar unto the LORD, and called upon the name of the LORD. Gen. 12: 8

The patriarchs and their households were nomadic and lived in tents, this is the evidence we have in our text and there is further evidence in Scripture. After the LORD appeared unto Abraham, we read [Gen. 26:25] "... He builded an altar there, and called upon the name of the LORD, and pitched his tent there..." Again we read of Jacob and Laban [Gen. 31:25] "Then Laban overtook Jacob. Now Jacob had pitched his tent in the mount: and Laban with his brethren pitched in the mount of Gilead." This did all the people of God from Abraham and during the journey to the Promised Land.

The term tent appears repeatedly in the Scriptures of both the Old and New Testaments, in the form of a covering, a dwelling place or a body. It is sometimes referred to as the "Tabernacle" or dwelling place for the "Ark of the Covenant," or the "Place of the Divine Presence."[1]

---

1 One of the significant glories of the promises of God is their eternal security to all who truly believe them. The Church affirms 'Lord, I belie ve, Lord, I believe, all things are possible...

In the Psalmist's view it was a place of security and worship [Psalm 27:5] "For in the time of trouble he shall hide me in his pavilion: in the secret of his tabernacle shall he hide me; he shall set me up upon a rock. And now shall mine head be lifted up above mine enemies round about me: therefore will I offer in the tabernacle sacrifices of joy; I will sing, yea, I will sing praises unto the LORD."

When the Presence of the LORD descended upon Balaam, he had a vision of the Almighty and said [Num. 24:5] "How godly are thy tents, O Jacob, and thy tabernacles O Israel." But there is another lesson that followed, something happened in another tent that caused defeat. Permit me to divert for a little while.

When the Philistines prevailed in the war against Israel, the "Ark of the Covenant" was captured and thirty thousand soldiers were killed, the rest retreated in panic to their tents not knowing why the battle had gone so badly wrong [1 Sam. 4:10] "...the Philistines fought, and Israel was smitten, and they fled every man to his tent: and there was a very great slaughter; for there fell of Israel thirty thousand footmen." Including two of the sons of the priest Eli.

Artificial righteousness always invites death and destruction. The Church always loses when waging war without God's Presence. The Church should have no battles of its own. The Church should not make convenience of spirituality. The Church should know that it is more dangerous to patronize the Presence of God than to oppose it. The Church should know that God is not afraid of abasing His people before their enemies, if they break His commandments.

The Contaminated Garment in the Tent:

When Joshua had inquired before God what had gone wrong: the LORD God said [Josh. 7:10] "...Get thee up: wherefore liest thou upon thy face? Israel hath sinned, and they have transgressed my covenant which I commanded them: for they have even taken of the accursed thing, and have also stolen, and dissembled also, and they have put it among their own stuff." The LORD will not have a mixed host, divided hearts, or the pure mixing with the impure.[2]

The LORD said [v.12-13] "... the children of Israel could not stand before their enemies, because they were accursed: neither will I be with you any more, except ye destroy the accursed thing from among you..." He told them to sanctify themselves for the future. There is an accursed thing in the midst of thee, O Israel: thou canst not stand before thine enemy, until ye take away the accursed thing." The LORD God has established a sovereign detective system in the moral universe.

---

2 The Babylonish brought defeat and disaster to Israel; the unclean thing will still bring failure and disaster to Christian individuals and congregations.

In God's dealing with His Church, you cannot do wrong and get right. What is done in secret and in darkness, cannot escape the gaze of the Holy Spirit. There are no paid detectives which God employees to detect the vulgarity of crime; but there are spiritual and ethical tests and criticisms, which will haunt a sinful man or woman to their doom. There are times when we must come before God man by man, woman by woman, facing the Eternal and answering the Omniscient.[3]

When the people were brought before Joshua, tribe by tribe, Achan of the tribe of Judah, the tribe out of which Jesus Christ would come, owned up and Joshua said unto him [Josh. 7:19-22] "...My son, give, I pray thee, glory to the God of Israel, and make confession unto him; and tell me now what thou hast done; hide it not from me.

And Achan answered Joshua, and said, Indeed I have sinned against the LORD God of Israel, and thus and thus have I done: When I saw among the spoils a goodly Babylonish garment, and two hundred shekels of silver, and a wedge of gold of fifty shekels weight, that I coveted them, and took them; and, behold, they are hid in the earth in the midst of my tent, and the silver under it. So Joshua sent messengers, and they ran into the tent; and

---

3   Abram was in constant communication with the LORD. One of the problems that we face as Christians is that we do not communicate with the Lord enough. We must also communicate with our culture without identifying with its values.

34

behold, it was hid in his tent, and the silver under it."

In confession to God, the sinner is invited to make a clean breast of his evil past. Let me hasten to say, it is a dangerous thing to moralize upon Achan and secretly attempt to repeat his sin. Here I end my diversion.

On his pilgrimage the historian said of the patriarch [Gen. 12:8] "And he removed from thence unto a mountain on the east of Bethel, and pitched his tent, having Bethel on the west, and Hai on the east: and there he builded an altar unto the LORD, called upon the name of the LORD." Mission in Canaan was that of a witness for the LORD.

For Abram the altar was a place of prayer, praise and sacrifice, it was a public testimony of his faith in God. The words of Jesus Christ to His disciples are so appropriate here [Acts 1:8] "...ye shall be witnesses unto me both in Jerusalem, and in all Judea, and in Samaria, and unto the utmost part of the earth."

Programme Declared:

There are two lessons to be learnt from Abram's actions: [1] by pitching his tent he declared himself a pilgrim and a stranger, he was there transiently and not permanently; he was on route to somewhere else – living by faith. [2] By building an altar he testified to a living faith in the LORD God. While the people of Canaan watched as spectators, it must have dawned on them that he had a personal relationship with a God who intervened when asked.

They must also have been moved in the belief of the holiness of Almighty God. The altar he built spoke of the absolute other-worldliness of God. God is holy and could only be approached through the atoning blood. The Christian life also is to bear this kind of testimony in today's world; as all the servants of God mentioned in the Hebrew Epistle chapter eleven, known as the "Catalogue of faith."[4]

Unashamed Confidence:

Abram's confidence in the faithfulness of God is shared by other saints. Some of them are listed in the chapter mentioned above. In prayer David said [Psalm 31:1] "In thee, O LORD do I put my trust; let me never be ashamed: deliver me in thy righteousness." Abram unashamedly built his altar in the presence of a heathen people in a heathen country. By doing so, he declared his anticipation and expectation of the fulfilment of the Divine promise.

The apostle Paul must have shared the same confidence in the promise he received on the road between Damascus and Jerusalem, he declared [Rom. 1:16] "For it is the power of God unto salvation to everyone that believeth; to the Jew first, and also to the Greek." Sometimes Christians are ashamed to declare their faith in Jesus Christ lest they

---

4   'O Jesus I have promised to serve Thee to the end, Be Thou forever near me, my Master and my Friend.'

should be ridiculed and be criticised, even lose their job or status in society.

According to the history of the "Primitive Church" and the "Early Church," this happened frequently during the first century of the Church and the ridicule and criticism have never ceased Christian. Unashamed confidence in the faithfulness of God's promise was costly in Abram's time and it is costly today. Would you take some time out to contemplate the:

Material Costliness
Moral Costliness
Educational Costliness
Political Costliness
Sacrificial Costliness
Religious Costliness
Social Costliness

Consider again the costliness that Abraham was commanded to make, "Get thee out of thy country, and from thy kindred, and from thy father's house, unto a land that I will show thee."

The Absolute Claim:

Abram had to make an absolute surrender to the sovereign claim of God. He pitched his tent and made an altar and the things of the altar. His primary function and focus, according to Auctor was to obey God and see the fulfilment of the promise [Heb. 11:9-10] "By faith he sojourned in the land of promise, as in a strange country, dwelling in tabernacles with Isaac and Jacob, the heirs with him of the same promise: For he looked for a city which hath foundations, whose builder and maker is God." [5]

The Christian who understands that the tent must be pitched in the right place to be a testimony and the altar must be built and function as a place of praise, prayer and worship; will gladly and willingly surrender all to Almighty God.

It is my fervent prayer that every Christian travel forward in the understanding of awesome command of God, the purified tent, holy altar and the ultimate sacrifice lifted up on Calvary's middle cross. Press along saints, the fullness of the promise is almost in sight.

---

5 The Christian is a debtor to God, every day that he or she lives.

THE SOJOURN IN EGYPT

There was a famine in the land: and Abram went down into Egypt to sojourn there; for the famine was grievous in the land. Gen. 12:10

The words of this text describe scenes that are beyond the imagination and experiences of the people who live in affluent western societies. But there are times however, when the scenes of abject poverty and destitution are brought into our homes through the medium of television and other channels of the media by means of technology. With famine come anger, hunger, disease, distress and death.

It is in the time of famine that we see the law of the jungle at its worst and we hear some of the oldest clichés in our language "The survival of the fittest; every man for himself; Don't cut off your nose to spoil your face; The bird in hand is worth more than a dozen in the bushes; Don't exchange bone for promise." Famine tests our character and our determination to survive.

The words of our text appear repeatedly in the same form and in different form throughout the Scripture and there is something, dark and dismal about them. Before we consider the wider implications of famine, our text reveals two distinct kinds: the first is spiritual and the second is material. In the spiritual world of our Christian Faith, as well as in the material of provisions and supply, changes in the weather conditions may come suddenly and unexpectedly.[1]

In the spiritual world, who would have thought that a man of Abram's calling, experience and faith, a man who was enjoined to God by covenant relationship would yield to the first temptation by which he was confronted? But before anyone of us dares to point the finger of condemnation, let me hasten to say, at our best and strongest moments we are in danger of falling, if we are not living in absolute obedience to God's commandments.

The Testing of Faith:

For the man called by God to a "Faith Pilgrimage," to experience grievous famine along the way was a great trial of faith. But for faith to triumph it must go through a process and be tried and tested. The apostle Peter, when speaking to the members of the "Early Church" said [1 Pet. 1:3, 7] "Blessed be the God and Father of our Lord Jesus Christ, which according to his abundant mercy hath begotten us again unto a lively hope by the resurrection of Jesus Christ from the dead... That the trial of your faith, being much more precious than of gold that perisheth, though it be tried with fire, might be found unto the

---

1   Gen. 26:1; 41:53-56; Ruth 1:1; 2 Sam. 21:1; 1 Kings 17:1; 2 Kings 4:18; Amos 8:11; Acts 11:28-29

praise and honour and glory at the appearing of Jesus Christ."

This kind of exhortation comes by experience and faith, faith has to lay hold on things unseen, of faith, Auctor says [Heb. 11:1] "Faith is the substance of things hoped for the evidence of things not seen." It is after great blessings that severe famine presents itself. It is here also that the greatest thirst is experienced and the greatest pangs of hunger are felt.

It is here too that men, even a man of Abram's faith had to make a decision. But that decision took him outside of the directive, will of God. The directive will of God always leads forward and upward.[2]

The Failure:

The second clause in our text reads "... Abram went down into Egypt to sojourn there." These words constitute the confession of defeat and failure. God had not failed, but Abram was in the wrong place, at the wrong time and in the wrong condition – he was apolulos. He had lost his way. An unknown author has left us with this question, "The last time you failed, did you stop trying because you failed – or did you fail because you stopped trying?

It may have seemed to Abram that God had failed, as

---

2   The Christians refer to the 'Will of God' in three ways: (1) The Omissive Will (2) The Persuasive Will (3) The Directive Will

it so often seems to us in the famine of our Christian experiences. What happened? Abraham had been focusing more on the land than on the God of promise; he was focusing on the blessing than on the Blesser. This is something that God prohibits. As Christians, our eyes must not be focused on the gifts but on the Giver. We must keep our eyes on Jesus Christ.

> There is an old hymn I learnt in Sunday school, some of the words read: "Turn your eyes upon Jesus, Look full in His wonderful face, And the things of this world, Will grow strangely dim, In the light of His glory and grace.

You do not have to treat your failure as a defeat, but as an experience of learning how.

The Downward Step:

The weakness and failure of anointed men come when they confuse and try to supplement providence – the continued activity of God with human wisdom. What did this stepping down from God's standard lead to?

The Fear:

Fear is said to be "The oldest and strongest emotion of mankind." It led Abram to believe that he would be killed, so as he and his kinsfolk drew near to Egypt he planned to deny his full relationship to Sarai. The Scripture bears record to his premeditated plan, he said to his wife [v.11]

"Behold now, I know that thou art a fair woman to look upon. Therefore it shall come to pass, when the Egyptians shall see thee, that they shall say, This is his wife: and they will kill me, but they will save you alive. Say I pray thee, thou art my sister: that it may be well with me for thy sake; and my soul shall live because of thee."

Abram had become afraid and his courage was gone from him. No people can become more fearful and weak than those who have turned aside from the life of faith. Those Christians who live in obedience to God's command, can be reassured by the words of the apostle Paul [2 Tim. 1:7] "God hath not given to us the spirit of fear; but of power, and of love and of a sound mind."

To another patriarch battling with the difficulties of his "Faith journey" the Word of the LORD came saying [Josh. 1:7] "Only be thou strong and very courageous, that thou mayest observe to do according to all the law, which Moses my servant commanded thee: turn not from it to the right hand or to the left, that thou mayest prosper whithersoever thou goest." Fear is a ubiquitous monster that has sought to paralyse the people of God since the dawn of creation.[3]

When the Hebrew people were overwhelmed with fear as they stood by the Red Sea, they challenged Moses and doubted the promises of God because of fear. Enveloped

---

3 Ps.. 5:7; 19:9; Luke 21:26; 2 Tim. 1:7

in their fear they said to Moses [Exodus 11-13] "Because there were no graves in Egypt, hast thou taken us away to die in the wilderness? Wherefore has thou dealt thus with us, and carry us forth out of Egypt?

Is not his the word that we did tell thee in Egypt, saying, Let us alone, that we may serve the Egyptians? For it had been better for us to serve the Egyptians than that we should die in wilderness, ... Moses said to the people "fear ye not, stand still, and see the salvation of the LORD, which he will show you today." Does your Red Sea seem uncrossable today? Are Pharaoh and his army closing in on you as a redeemed child of God? The solution is – stand still and see the salvation of the LORD.

When young David stood before the giant Goliath and the Philistine Army. The heart of the Israelite soldiers were gripped with fear and the Philistine giant asked [1 Sam. 17:43] "Am I a dog, that thou comest to me with staves? And the Philistine cursed David by his gods ..., he said to David "Come to me, and I will give thy flesh unto the fowls of the air, and to the beasts of the field..., David said to the Philistine, thou comest to me with a sword, and with a spear, and with a shield: but I come to thee in the name of the LORD God of hosts, the God of the armies of Israel, whom thou hast defied." Christians who live by the commandment of God can say to their Goliath "I come to you in the name of the LORD God of hosts."

The Selfishness:

One of the primary laws of human nature is self-protection. Most people will protect themselves at any cost. According to our text, Abram was more concerned about his own safety than the chastity and honour of his wife. He said to Sarai [v.13] "Say, I pray thee, that thou art my sister; that it may be well with me for thy sake; and my soul shall live because of thee." When a man turns away from God, his interest is sure to become centred on himself.

It was true about Abram when he stepped down from the standard ordained by God and it is still true for Christians today. When a man or a woman steps down from the ordained standard of God, fear will grip the heart like nothing else can. When Saul sought the life of David because of jealousy, he knew that he had slipped from the standard that God had commanded him to keep.

When he heard where David was hiding, he took an army of men to destroy him, but David knew that fear led to selfishness and death. His testimony was [Psalm 23:4] "... though I walk through the valley of the shadow of death, I will fear no evil." Again, he testified in another place [Psalm 27:1] "The LORD is my light and my salvation. Whom shall I fear? The LORD is the strength of my life of whom shall I be afraid?"

Saul was so overwhelmed with hatred and jealousy

in pursuing David that he and his whole army became drunken with intoxicating sleep and the LORD showed David where Saul had pitched. The historian wrote [1 Sam. 26:5] "David arose and came to the place where Saul had pitched: and David beheld the place where Saul lay, and Abner the son of Ner, the captain of his host: and Saul lay in the trench, and the people pitched round about him."

David had no fear in him for he knew that the LORD was on his side, so he asked the question "Who will go down with me to Saul's camp?" and Abashai volunteered. "I will go down with thee." When they reached where Saul was, Abashai said [v.9] "God hath delivered thine enemy into thine hand this day: now therefore let me smite him, I pray thee, even to the earth at once, and I will not smite him the second time."

There are times when Christians are caught up with the spirit of fatalism. They boil over with anger and revenge; they come to their jealous, weary and sleeping Saul and Say: let us destroy him, for God hath delivered him into our hands. Like Abashai, Christians can be driven by anger and revenge. But David who understood the command of God said [v.9] "Destroy him not" then he added this question "...Who can stretch forth his hand against the LORD'S anointed, and be guiltless?[4]

After Saul realised that David had come into his camp,

---

4 Prov. 1:17; 14:9; Jer. 17:11; Rom. 1:22; Eph. 5:15

taken away his sword and water as evidence but spared his life. He said [1 Sam. 26:21] "Behold, I have played the fool, and have erred exceedingly." When a person steps out of God's will he can become angry and fearful; fear then leads to jealousy and Jealousy leads to foolishness and foolishness leads to selfishness – especially when people are shouting "Saul has slain his thousands but David, his ten thousands."

In the world of theology a fool is described as: one who is rash and unreasonable: the term often refers to one who is not mentally retarded but who is lacking in moral qualities.

The Hypocrisy:

It is without controversy that hypocrisy can plunge the mind of a man into a dark abyss, when he believes his own self-flattery instead of God's ordained purpose. Abram pretended to be what he was not.

Sarai was the wife of Abraham by the covenant of marriage and she was also his half-sister. He convinced Sarai to commit herself to his deliberate misrepresentation. This is the next step to the backslider, pretending not to be what he truly was. However advanced a man may be in his Christian service, experience and age; he is still in danger of falling.

There is abundant evidence to support this, consider

for example Solomon of Jerusalem the wisest man that ever lived. [1 Kings 3:3-28]. Indeed the Scripture says [3:30] "Solomon's wisdom excelled the wisdom of all the children of the east country and all the wisdom of Egypt..., And he spoke [wrote] three thousand proverbs and his songs were a thousand and five..., And there came of all people to hear the wisdom of Solomon, from all the kings of the earth, which had heard of his wisdom."[5]

He was blessed and guided by God in the following chapters, then we read some of the saddest words in all of Scripture [1 Kings 11:1,3,6] "But Solomon loved many strange women, together with the daughter of Pharaoh, women of the Moabities, Ammonites, Edomites, Zidionians and Hittites...; And he had seven hundred wives, princes and three hundred concubines, and his wives turned away his heart...; And Solomon did evil in the sight of the LORD, and went not fully after the LORD ..."
...

He continued to pretend that he was the anointed king of Israel, but the historic, spiritual and practical evidence showed that he was a great pretender. John Milton observed: "For neither man nor angel can discern hypocrisy, the only evil that walks invisibly, except to

---

5 Jude warned the Christians of his time not to compromise their faith as Abram did, but to 'keep themselves in the love of God, looking for the mercy of our Lord Jesus Christ unto eternal life (Jude v.18).

God alone. By His permissive will, through Heav'n and earth. And oft through wisdom wake, suspicion sleeps at wisdom's gate, and to simplicity, resigns her charge, while goodness thinks no evil seems." The Christian cannot afford to live one-way in private and another way in public. Jesus rebuked the deeply religious Pharisees for their hypocrisy when He said [Matt. 23:23]

> *"Woe unto you, teachers of the law and Pharisees, you hypocrites! For ye pay tithe of mint and anise and cumin, and have omitted the weightier matters of the law, judgment, mercy, and faith: these ought ye to have done, and not leave the other undone."*

Then He challenged them in the following words:

"Ye blind guides, which strain at a gnat, and swallow a camel: Woe unto you, scribes and Pharisees, hypocrites! For ye make clean the outside of the cup and of the platter, but within they are full of extortion and excess. Thou blind Pharisee cleanse thou that which is within the cup and platter, that the outside of them may be clean also. Woe unto you scribes and Pharisees, hypocrites! For ye are like unto whited sepulchres, which indeed appear beautiful outward, but are within full of dead men bones, and of all uncleanness. Even so ye also outwardly appear righteous unto men, but within ye are full of hypocrisy and iniquity."[6]

---

6   Jesus was uncompromising in telling the Pharisees and

Hypocrisy is a contaminating disease that is diagnosed by everyone else, except the person who has it. Disobedience to the command of God led Abraham into hypocrisy.

Open Rebuke:

Every man and woman needs to be corrected or rebuked at some point in life, but more than all every person who calls upon the name of the LORD needs to be rebuked when they step out of righteousness into unrighteousness, whether they be king or citizen, president or senator, prince or pauper, prophet or priest, caterer or cleaner, pope or cardinal or in whatever category of life they find themselves. Speaking of friendship and rebuke, Solomon wrote [27:5-6] "Open rebuke is better than secret love. Faithful are the wounds of a friend; but the kisses of an enemy are deceitful."

After the LORD had sent plagues upon Pharaoh and his house because of Sarai Abram's wife. Pharaoh called Abram and said, "What is this that thou hast done unto me? Why didst thou not tell me that she was thy wife...?" It is an awful thing when the ungodly have to rebuke the godly.

Christians should not refuse to rebuke correct or, rebuke others who have fallen into sin and help them to true repentance and restoration. The Scripture however, gives

---

Sadducees the truth. Scripture says: 'You shall know the truth, and the truth shall make you free.'

us instructions as to how we rebuke and restore people in righteousness. In the Book of Samuel, we read how the prophet Nathan rebuked David. He skilfully used a parable to point out David's sin and transgression. David listened carefully to the case clothed in the diplomatic presentation of a parable. He became angry and hastily passed judgment upon the villain whom Nathan described.

Nathan was a brave, righteous and wise prophet; he was brave because he was confronting a king who had the power to take his life; he was righteous because he did not allow injustice and position to cloud his judgment; and he was wise for using a parable that David could easily understand being a former shepherd. The king on the other hand made a rash judgment. There are times when we as Christians act rashly and hastily; we pass judgment even when we do not know whom the person we are hearing about is. So what lessons can we learn from this story?

Part of the story recorded by the historian says [2 Sam. 12:5-7] "David's anger was greatly kindled against the man; And he said to Nathan, As the LORD liveth, the man that hath done this thing shall surely die..., And Nathan said to David, Thou art the man..., The LORD said "Behold, I will raise up evil against thee out of thine own house..., What you did, you did in secret, but what I am about to do, I will do openly before all Israel and before the sun." God's righteousness will not allow sin to go unpunished.

In our modern, liberal, sophisticated society, we do not like to use the word sin and when righteous preachers preach against sin and unrighteousness from the Holy pulpit, even some members of the church become angry and upset. The preachers can see their faces and read their body language and observe their discomfort, the righteous preacher can hear their negative gossip. But the righteous preachers have a mandate to live righteously and preach righteousness; even if he is driven out of town or out of the church.[7]

Responding to Rebuke:

When David discovered that he was the guilty man; the man he had sentenced to death, he urgently sought the forgiveness and mercy of God. David knew that his position as king of Israel did not make him immune from the judgment of God. He was conscious that Satan had instilled his poison in his life and had fanned the flames of his corrupt and lustful desires within his heart. He was not dragged by any external force to the commission of sin, but his own flesh enticed him and he willingly yielded to its allurements.

There is a common belief in our world today that mere time cancels out and removes the guilt of sin. To believe this is to deny the doctrine of Holy Scripture. The real

---

7 Forgiveness brings the whole of God into our life and the whole of our life into the presence of God.

truth is that in essence, sin is the abuse of the free will, the misuse of what is good. The basis of all sin is self-righteousness. It was so with Abram and with David and it is the same with us today.

David's attitude to the rebuke of the prophet Nathan was to repent and seek the mercy of God. His prayer of repentance is to be found in the Psalter. Together we can reflect on it [Psalm 51:1-11*ff*]

> *"Have mercy upon me, O God, according to thy lovingkindness, according unto the multitude of thy tender mercies blot out my transgressions. Wash me thoroughly from mine iniquities, and cleanse me from my sin. For I acknowledge my transgressions: and my sin is ever before me. Against thee, thee only, have I sinned, and done this evil in thy sight: that thou mightiest be justified when thou speakest, and be clear when thou judgest. Behold, I was shapen in iniquity; and in sin did my mother conceive me. Behold, thou desirest truth in the inward parts: and in the hidden part thou shalt make me to know wisdom. Purge me with hyssop, and I shall be clean: wash me, and I shall be whiter than snow. Make me to hear joy and gladness; that the bones which thou hast broken may rejoice. Hide not thy face from my sins, and blot out all mine iniquities. Create in me a clean heart, O God; and renew a right spirit within me..."*

Both Abram and David realised that their secret sin on

earth was open scandal in heaven. What about you and me?

The Contagion:

The LORD interposed mysteriously because of Sarai; the historian wrote [v.17] "And the LORD plagued Pharaoh and his house with great plagues because of Sarai Abraham's wife." The plague of divine judgment will no doubt fall upon many because of the unfaithfulness of many of God's believing people. In His message to His disciples, Jesus said [Matt. 5:16] "Let your light so shine before men, that they may see your good works, and glorify your Father which is in heaven."

Since we are interdependent on one another, no one of us can sin without it having an impact on someone else, or as Christians, we cannot live for the Lord without it having an impact on others. John Bunyan said "One leak will sink a ship one sin will destroy a sinner." Abram's not only brought trouble on himself and Sarai, it brought the plagues upon Pharaoh and his household. [8]

John Alexander who partnered with me in delivering two lectures on the "Biblical Nature of Sin" and "The Theological Nature of Sin," said "Sin and repentance are the only grounds for hope and joy; the grounds for reconciled joyful relationships. You can be born again."

---

8 Ps. 78:4; Joel 2:23-27

This is the beginning of the way out of Egypt.

Restoration:

The words [Gen. 13:1] "...And Abram went up out of Egypt, he, and his wife, and all that he had, and Lot went with him, into the south." Keep in mind these words [Gen. 12:1] "Get thee out of thy country." [12:10] "Abram went down into Egypt." [13:1] "Abram went up out of Egypt." These three stages and the entrance into Canaan were of the utmost importance for his restoration.

He went out of Ur of the Chaldea
He went down into Egypt
He went up out of Egypt
He went into Canaan

Abram was conscious that he had lost his integrity and character when he went down into Egypt. He was obedient to God when he was commanded to "get out of his country." Now he was in the process of restoration as he "went up out of Egypt." The way to restoration is the way upward. David was uniquely aware of this when he said [Psalm 121:1-2] "I will lift up mine eyes unto the hills, from whence cometh my help. My help cometh from the LORD, which made heaven and earth."

The real servant of God makes a poor sinner. Abram did not build an altar in Egypt. Experientially there is no fellowship with God while we walk by sight and not by faith. The true and only remedy for sin is to return to the place of the altar – the Cross of Jesus Christ. This is the place of repentance, forgiveness, restoration, communion and rededication that leads to consecration.

Earlier I said, the prodigal son had to return to father and home from whom he had wandered [Luke 15]. Restoration was promised to all of God's backslidden children when He inspired His prophet to say [Jer. 3:22-23] "Return, ye backsliding children, and I will heal your backslidings. Behold, we come unto thee; for thou art the LORD our God. Truly in vain is salvation hoped for from the hills, and from the multitude of mountains: truly in the LORD our God is the salvation of Israel." This promise of restoration and consecration is relevant to you and me today. Will you return to the LORD our God?

THE MAN OF PEACE

The experiences and history of Abram's sojourn recorded in this section of the story is fascinating, relevant and significant for Christians today. In typology his wisdom and maturity in dealing with his nephew Lot and his herdsmen relates to two different kinds of Christian. Lot was a covenant maker and keeper, in other words he was a righteous man.

The report we have of him shows that he lived by sight and sense. His mind was focused on worldly pleasure and the maximization of profit he had become intoxicated with material things. He is the type of un-consecrated Christian, whose riches increased and he set his heart on it. One who had neglected the altar and forfeited Divine Guidance.

On the other hand, Abram lived by faith and trusted the promises of God. He built an altar and attended to the things of the altar. In going up out of Egypt and returning to Canaan the Scripture says he returned [13:4] "Unto the place of the altar, which he had made there at the first: and there Abram called on the name of the LORD." He had faltered but not failed like Lot. Abram was not unhelpful towards Lot and there is no record that Lot built any altar.[1]

---

1 Gen 13:5-18; Deut. 32:25; Rom. 12:17-21

The consecrated Abram could not live without worship, while the un-consecrated Lot did. There is no doubt that the well- watered plains had more attraction to Lot and still has for the worldly believers. But for Abram the altar was embraced in thanksgiving and worship, what we have come to recognise as "The Higher Christian Life." This is to fix one's hopes on things eternal.

The Impossible Relationship:

Almost all human relationships begin and most of them continue as forms of mutual exploitation, a kind of mental or physical barter, to be terminated when one or both parties find it impossible to maintain the mutuality. Some people have confessed that the easiest kind of relationship for them is with ten thousand people and the hardest is with one person.

In the relationship of Abram and Lot, prosperity had its social troubles! Not property only, but landed property and livestock innumerable. What is clearly revealed here is that wealth has its hindrances and its embarrassment. The Scripture says [Gen. 13:6] "... the land was not able to bear them, that they might dwell together: for their substance was great, so that they could not dwell together."[2]

In other words, the condition of the country had a central

2 The gift of choice carries two significant things (1) privilege (2) responsibility

part in their being able to dwell together. Keep in mind that Abram was being guided by "heavenly wisdom" and Lot by "worldly wisdom." The core element that held their relationship together had gradually disappeared – mutuality. People are interested in others if others are interested in them.

Even the "Land of Promise" was not able to sustain such an unequal yoke as the life of faith in God and the life of sense and worldly wisdom. Note carefully the words of the biblical historian [v.7] "And there was strife between the herdmen of Abram's cattle and the herdmen of Lot's cattle and the Canaanite and the Perizzite dwelt in the land."

This is the kind of strife that takes up residence in a Christian heart. It is the conflict between the fleshly life [sark] and the spiritual life [pneumatikos]. As long as the strife continues the land of promise [the Church] seems to yield no blessings. Paul alluded to this in his epistle to the Romans [7], where he wrote about [1] The law of sin [2] The problem of indwelling sin and [3] The wrestling of two natures. Carnal Christians like Lot, put no value on the sovereign promise of God.

Magnanimity the true wealth:

There is nothing in this world that can be equalled to the generosity of the Christian faith. Abram's generosity was a demonstration and an effective lesson that great

Christians should have generous faith. To the generous Christian, faith is not knowing what the future holds, but knowing who holds the future and who owns the land.

In his conversation with Lot to end the strife, Abram did two things [v. 8-9] 1. He asked Lot the question "Is not the whole land before thee? 2. He gave him a choice "If thou wilt take the left hand, then I will go to the right." The person who truly knows God can be generous and let others have the first choice. The land on the left hand and the land on the right hand are both God's property and either would do for the man of God.

The servant of God must not strive. As Christians, we can show our trust in God by standing back from the strife of tongue and by allowing others to occupy the chief seats. Let us stand up for God and be generous in the exercise of our faith. The God that stood up for Abram's right will stand up for our rights and will keep His promise to us.

John Ruskin said, "Lately in a wreck off a California ship, one of the passengers fastened a belt about him with two hundred pounds of gold in it, with which he was found afterward at the bottom. Now, as he was sinking – had he the gold? Or had the gold him?

The Carnal Mind:

The carnal mind has surrendered to the popular drift with an absolute weakness and nerve-less-ness unmatched in selfish history. This was demonstrated in Lot's attitude response to Abram's questions. The opportunity to choose and the promise [13:10-11] "Lot lifted up his eyes, and beheld all the plain of Jordan, that it was well watered everywhere, before the LORD destroyed Sodom and Gomorrah even as the garden of the LORD, like the land of Egypt, as thou camest unto Zoar.[3]

Then Lot chose him all the plain of Jordan; and Lot journeyed east: and they separated themselves the one from the other." Little did Lot know what he was choosing with his carnal mind. He saw only the outside of the place. He selected his residence without moral inquiry, for even a well-watered place will not save sinners from the judgement of God.

Lot was driven by a lusting and a thirst for power and wealth. The Christian is instructed not to abandon the promise of God for luxury, for the lust for luxury is more destructive than any enemy. Lot looked for the best things and chose them and never expressed gratitude or said thanks. He separated himself from Abram – the man of faith with an ungrateful heart.

Carnal Christians do not set great value on the fellowship of a holy man. Lot's mind was focused on earthly prosperity, not on heavenly things. Jesus warned the

---

3 Luke 16:19-31 – Jesus told the story of a man with a carnal mind. He was so enveloped in himself that he treated a poor beggar as insignificant.

people of His day [Matt. 6:19] "Lay not up for yourselves treasures upon earth, where moth and rust doth corrupt, and where thieves break through and steal: for where your treasures are there will your heart be also."

The question must be asked and answered, how much did Lot gain by separating himself from Abram? He pitched his tent in Sodom and Gomorrah and there is no record that he built an Altar there, neither is there any record that he made provision to spend time with God. In the end, he was driven out of Sodom by fire. It was Raymond Dale who observed "I am having more trouble with myself than any other man I have ever met."

The Spiritual Mind:

The entrepreneur and novelist Alexander Graham Bell wrote "When one door closes another door opens; but we so often look so long and so regretfully upon the door, that we do not see the ones which opens for us." After the separation from Lot, a door of opportunity was closed. Abram could no longer advise him or support him as he did in the past and that was a painful blow to Abram and for Lot in later years.

However, Abram did not sink into the valley of bitterness, despair, helplessness and hopelessness, believing that he had invested his life in caring for a younger relative, who was enticed away by the lust and thirst for material things and closed the door on their relationship. One of the lessons that we learn from this story is that Abram saw a new door opened to him as he continued to believe the promises of God.

The LORD spoke to him and said [13:14] "... Lift up now thine eyes, and look from the place where thou art northward, and southward, and eastward, and westward: for all the land which thou seest, to thee will I give it, and to thy seed for ever." Note after separation came the message of comfort, hope and promise.

In Paul's plea to the Corinthian believers to separate themselves from unbelievers quoting words from the Pentateuchal historian [Lev.26:12] "...I will walk among you, and will be your God, and ye shall be my people." [Jer. 31:33] "But this shall be the covenant that I will make with the house of Israel; after these days, saith the LORD, I will put my law in their inward parts, and write it in their hearts: and will be their God, and they shall be my people."

In later years Paul spoke to the Christians at Corinth saying [2 Cor. 6:8] "Wherefore come out from among them, and be ye separate, saith the Lord, and touch not the unclean thing: and I will receive you, and be a Father unto you, and ye shall be my sons and daughters, saith the Lord Almighty."

It was covetousness and material greed, which caused Lot to "Lift up his eyes." But Abram lifted up his eyes at the invitation of the LORD. It is in this that we find the difference between the carnal Christian and the spiritual Christian. Lot was enticed by worldly lust and self-interest, Abram was moved by the Word of God. Looking up were the watchwords of the servant of God and they are the watchwords of the Christians. They must form and inform the attitude of every person who is separated unto the LORD. Lot was guided by his own understanding, while Abram held steadfastly to the promises of God.

In the absolute surrender of his life to Jesus Christ from Phariseeism Paul said to the Christians of Galatia [Gal.2:20] "I am crucified with Christ: nevertheless I live; yet not I, but Christ liveth in me: and the life which I now live in the flesh I live by the faith of the Son of God, who loved me, and gave himself for me." It was Aldous Huxley who left us with this observation "Experience is not what happens to a man, it is what a man does with what happens to him.

The Altar of Testimony:

In continuing his journey, the Scripture says [Gen. 13:18] "Then Abram removed his tent, and came and dwelt in the plain of Mamre, which is in Hebron, and built there an altar unto the LORD." The difference between these two men was poles apart. Lot pitched his tent toward Sodom; Abram pitched his tent in the city of refuge. The self-seeking Christian bears no testimony for God. When he becomes conscious of God, his words are treated with mockery.

There is clear evidence of this in Lot's warning to his sons-in-law [Gen.19:14] "Lot went out, and spake unto his sons-in -law, which married his daughters, and said, Up, get you out of this place; for the LORD will destroy this city, but they seemed as one that mocked unto his sons-in-law. Over time, Lot's testimony degenerated to the place where even his family did not believe that his warning was serious.

On the other hand Abram testified about God by building Altars, as did the patriarch Noah before him [Gen. 8:20] "...Noah builded an altar unto the LORD; and took of every clean beast, and of every clean fowl and offered burnt offerings on the altar." Brother Lawrence left us with these encouraging words "We should dedicate ourselves to become in this life the most perfect worshippers of God we can possibly be, as we hope to be through all eternity. We can now join Francis of Assisi in prayer:

Lord, make me an instrument of your peace, Where there is hatred, let me sow love; Where there is injury, pardon; Where there is doubt, faith; Where there is despair, hope; Where there is darkness, light; Where there is sadness joy.

O Divine Master, grant that I may not so much seek; To be consoled as to console; Not so much to be understood as to understand; Not so much to be loved as to love; For it is in giving that we receive; It is in pardoning that we are pardoned; It is in dying that we are born to eternal life. Amen.

THE FAITHFUL MAN

Abram responded positively to the call of God and left the country of his birth, not certain of where he was going. According to the historian [12:4] "He departed, as the LORD had spoken unto him; and Lot went with him..." In a sense, Abram followed the LORD, and Lot followed Abram. With his desire set on material plenty, Lot soon found a new dwelling place in Sodom, where he became a captive. His lust for material plenty and worldly practices led him into spiritual bondage and social bondage and unexpected disaster. It is here that Abram's faith was demonstrated.

Consider with me six things about the character of the man of faith:

A Man of Compassion:

Compassion is pity and sympathy for someone who is in need. The gospels revealed that Jesus Christ, "was moved with compassion" repeatedly. But close examination of His ministry reveals something greater, it revealed empathy. The Greek New Testament renders it "eleos," meaning "mercy." There is abundant evidence in both the Old and New Testament that not all people are merciful or empathic.[1]

---

1   Jesus used the word 'certain' on four occasions – to position

The Gospel of Luke bears record of the "Parable of the Good Samaritan." [Luke 10:25-37] It is a parable that high-lighted five disturbing things which Jesus sought to correct:

Economic deprivation
Religious bigotry
Racial prejudice
Political inequality
Social divisions
The preamble to this parable carries two questions:
Master what shall I do to inherit eternal life?
Who is my neighbour?

To understand the theology of Jesus, we are duty bound to re-read the preamble, even the whole story. For our purpose here let us re-read five verses [Luke 10:25-29] "Behold, a certain lawyer stood up, and tempted him, saying, Master, what shall I do to inherit eternal life? He said unto him, What is written in the law? How readest thou? And he answering said, Thou shalt love the Lord thy God with all thy heart, and with all thy soul, and with all thy strength, and with all thy mind; and thy neighbour as thyself. And he said unto him, Thou hast answered right: this do, and thou shalt live. But he willing to justify himself, said unto Jesus, and who is my neighbour?"

---

this story in every age of time, in every country of the world and in every people group. It is a story without walls.

Jesus was never quick to give a yes or no answer, He had a way of challenging those who questioned Him, to question their own consciences and when they answered out of a good conscience, He would instruct them to practice righteousness. In this parable, Jesus spoke of the attitude and behaviour of four men.

A Certain Lawyer
A Certain Man
A Certain Priest
A Certain Samaritan

This lawyer was highly educated, profoundly religious, well respected and it seemed very popular in his community. In responding to his questions, "What is written in the law?" and "How readest thou? Jesus gave him top marks. Then Jesus said to him, "This do, and thou shalt live." But he was wrapped in self-righteousness and sought to justify himself, so he asked Jesus another question "Who is my neighbour?"

Jesus imprinted the story on his conscience [10:30-35], then asked him this arresting and compelling question [v.36] "Which now of these three, thinkest thou, was neighbour unto him that fell among thieves?" The lawyer had no way of escaping the truth of his own conscience, thus he answered [v.37] He that showed mercy on him: Jesus, then instructed him to practice what his conscience revealed. "...Go and do thou likewise." In other words, go and practice compassion. To do so the lawyer had to be deskilled from at least seven things:

Self-importance

Cultural Indifference
Historical Hatred
Racial Prejudice
Religious Bigotry
Spiritual Blindness
Theoretical Legalism

These were some of the things that hindered "the certain priest" and the "Levite" from extending compassion to "the certain wounded man." How about you and me today?

What can we, – Christians learn about compassion from this story? Compassion or empathy grows out of love for our neighbour. Who are our neighbours? As Christians, which wounded and dying persons have we made a sacrifice to help on our modern Jericho road in recent days? Whose cry have we heard and crossed over to the other side of the road? We did not want to get involved. Whose cry did we hear; went over to look and see if they were one of us and when they did not look like us, we crossed over the road and passed by?

Do we modern Christians have the right to pick and choose which wounded person we make a sacrifice for on our Jericho road? Are the same things that Jesus had to deskill this lawyer from preventing us from being whom God wants us to be? Do we need to be deskilled from our self-importance, racial prejudice, cultural indifference, religious bigotry, historical hatred, spiritual blindness and theoretical legalism?

Who is my neighbour? Every person in need is a neighbour. Love that is born at Calvary bears and fore-bears, gives and forgives. Mechtild Magdebury, wrote "Compassion means that if I see my friend and my enemy in equal need, I shall help both equally. Justice demands that we seek and find the stranger, the broken, prisoners and comfort them and offer them our help. Here lies the holy compassion of God."[2]

When Abram learnt that his nephew Lot was taken captive in the battle of the four kings [Gen.14:1-12] he could have responded negatively, but he did not. He immediately took a decision to go and help him. Those who truly walk with God cannot remain indifferent to human suffering wherever it exists.

A Man of Courage:

Abram and his servants had the courage to go to war against four kings and their armies. The man whom Lot had injured was now his deliverer. This was the true

---

2   We cannot serve God, except we serve Him sacrificially and faithfully.

retaliation of a man of compassion and courage. The scripture says [14:14-16] "...When Abram heard that his brother was taken captive, he armed his trained servants, born in his own house, three hundred and eighteen, and pursued them unto Dan."

There are four significant things that Abram did:

He armed his servants
He pursued the enemy
He overtook the enemy

He recovered and brought back Lot, his family and their property

He was a warrior and a pilgrim. Martin Luther King said "Courage is an inner resolution to go forward in spite of obstacles and frightening situations; cowardice is a submissive surrender to circumstance: courage breeds creative self-abnegation. Courage faces fear and thereby masters it; cowardice represses fear and is thereby mastered by it. Courageous men never lose the zest for living even though their life situation is zestless; cowardly men, overwhelmed by the uncertainties of life, lose the will to live."

What we learn from Abram's action is that the man of faith attempts great things through the power of God. The apostle Paul wrote [1 Cor. 1:27] "...God hath chosen the foolish things of the world to confound the wise; and God hath chosen the weak things of the world to confound the things which are mighty."

Abram's faith functioned by his relationship with God and his love for his nephew Lot, so he hazarded all to rescue him. Great faith constrains to attempt what seemed impossible. The missionary to India, William Carey said, "Expect great things from God, attempt great things for God."

The founder of the Salvation Army, William Booth, took this quite literally when he said "Faith and works should travel side by side, step answering to step, like the legs of man walking. First faith and then works; and then faith again, and then works again – until you can scarcely distinguish which is one from the other." Abram's faith was welded to his love for his nephew Lot and this made him a man of courage and positioned him alongside men of faith like Moses, Nehemiah and Paul. It was Paul who said [Phil. 4:13] "I can do all things through Christ who strengtheneth me."

A Man of Recovery:

Abram's action in pursuing and overtaking the enemy resulted in him recovering Lot, his family, others and their goods. The man of recovery is a man who truly believed in the Omnipotent God. He believed that God was able to do extra-ordinary things, like giving him the power to recover all that was lost.

The scripture says [Gen.14:16] "...he brought back all the goods, and also brought again his brother Lot and his goods, and the women also, and the people." Abram as a separated man dwelt in the presence of a Holy God. He went to war as a man who had come out from the holy, soul-inspiring presence of the LORD. He gained the victory when he had successfully completed the recovery of his family.

Lot, by living in Sodom had become part of a heathen people and he could not save himself. It was the separated one alone who was able to save others. Abram's ability to make the recovery was bound up in his life of faith. If we – the Christians – would have victory from God and through God, then we must be separated unto Him.

A Man of Liberation:

The theologian Karl Bath, speaking about trusting God, said "In God alone there is faithfulness and faith in the trust we may hold to Him. To hold God is to rely on the fact that God is there for me, and to live in this certainty." After rescuing Lot, Bera the king of Sodom went out to meet him in the valley Shaveh. Abram also met with Melchizedek, the king and priest of Salem.

The report of that latter meeting states [Gen. 14:18-20] "Melchizedek of Salem brought forth bread and wine: and he was the priest of the most high God. And he blessed him, and said, Blessed be Abram of the most high

God, possessor of heaven and earth: And blessed be the most high God, which hath delivered thine enemies into thine hand. And he gave him tithes of all." This was the beginning of Union and Communion.

We now return to the former meeting and its report [Gen. 14:21-23] "The king of Sodom said unto Abram, Give me the persons, and take the goods to thyself. And Abram said to the king of Sodom, I have lifted up mine hand unto the LORD, the most high God, the possessor of heaven and earth that I will not take from a thread even to a shoe lachet, and that I will not take any thing that is thine, lest thou shouldest say, I have made Abram rich: save only that which the young men have eaten, and the portion of the men which went with me. Aner, Eschol, and Mamre; let them take their portion."

Abram took what was offered to him by Melchizedek because he was the priest of the most high God, to which order of Priest, Jesus Christ, belongs. The Hebrew Epistle recorded the following words [Heb. 7:13] "...For he of whom these things are spoken pertaineth to another tribe, of which no man gave attendance at the altar.

For it is evident that our Lord sprang out of Judah; of which tribe Moses spoke nothing concerning priesthood. And it is yet far more evident: for that after the similitude of Melchizedek that there ariseth another priest. Who is made, not after the law of a carnal commandment, but after the power of an endless life. For he testifieth, Thou art a priest for ever after the order of Melchidezek."

What does this mean for the Christians? It means that Jesus Christ, the Priest of the Most High God, will so bless and refresh all who, like Abram go forth in His name to walk, work and to war. What a joy and privilege to meet the Blessing Priest when returning tired and weary from the struggle of faith! Many battles the separated man of God will need to fight on the behalf of family and others, but Jesus Christ the Sovereign and Succouring King of Peace, will meet him and with His help and blessing, and finally with His "Well Done," which will be the Eternal and Heavenly Benediction.

The hymn writer Lucy Campbell summed up for us when she penned four verses of a consoling hymn, two verses say:

> If when this life of labour is ended, And the reward of the race you have run; O the sweet rest that's prepared for the faithful, Will be His blest and final "Well done."

> But if you try, and fail in your trying, hands sore and scarred from the work you've begun; Take up your cross and run quickly to meet Him; He'll understand, He'll say "Well done."

The Assurance

After these things the word of the LORD came unto Abram in a vision, saying, Fear not, Abram: I [am] thy shield, [and] thy exceeding great reward. Gen. 15: 1

Throughout his pilgrimage, Abram had made the promises of God the glory of his life. His actions revealed the independence and dignity of true religion. He was at a place in his pilgrimage when he needed some words of assurance and consolation and the LORD sent words unto him saying [Gen. 15:1] "Fear not Abram: I am thy shield, and thy exceeding great reward." Abram needed these words to confirm earlier promises.

All of us, at some point in our lives need a word of assurance and confirmation. During the turbulent years of the sixteenth- century reformation, Martin Luther in a letter to Erasmus penned, "The Holy Spirit is no skeptic. He has written neither doubt nor mere opinion into our hearts, but rather solid assurances. Which are more sure and solid than all experience and even life itself." The man who truly ventures forth on the promises of God will not allow his assurance to depend upon his own powers of imagination. He knows that the LORD'S words are always in season. He is conscious that the LORD will speak a word in time of difficulty and weariness.

The Time of God's Assurance:

Reflect on the words of the text [Gen.15:1] "After these things the word of the LORD came unto Abram in a vision, saying, Fear not Abram, I am thy shield, and exceeding great reward." After the war against the four kings and the rescue of Lot, his family and goods were recovered; they were amazed at the miracle of God's salvation.

What Abram achieved by faith did not bring self-confidence, but a greater dependence on the LORD. Abram may well have feared that the defeated kings would have re-grouped and started a new war; he may well have questioned his own soul at refusing the gifts of the king of Sodom, but the LORD gave this assurance "Fear not Abram, I am the shield, and exceeding great reward." This brought complete consolation and comfort to Abram and those with him.

The Assurance of God's Security:

God uses a variety of ways to communicate His messages to mankind. The message came to Abram in a vision, assuring him that the rejection of the reward of the king of Sodom created the opportunity of a greater reward. When God offered Himself as Abram's reward, nothing else was needed and no reward could be greater. For where God guides, He also provides.[1]

---

1 The lamb on Mount Moriah; Elijah at brook Cherith; Hebrew people in the wilderness.

What lessons can Christians learn from this message to Abram? We can learn that a steadfast faith in the providence of God is the solution to all earthly problems. It may also be a sovereign truth that a full understanding of the universal providence of God is the solution of most theological misunderstandings.

In this message, there is the assurance of love and security. George Matheson, in a personal sense captured it in the following words "O Love that wilt not let me go, I rest my weary soul in Thee, I give Thee back the life I owe, That in Thy ocean depths it flow may richer fuller be." There is also another message that God gave to Jeremiah for the people of Israel [Jer. 33:2-3] "Thus saith the LORD the maker thereof, the LORD that formed it, to establish it; the LORD is his name; Call unto me, and I will answer thee, and show thee great and mighty things, which thou knowest not."

The messages to Abram and later to Israel are reminders to all Christians of the fullness and faithfulness of the blessings of Jesus Christ. "Fear not ... be of good cheer" John recorded the message of Jesus Christ [John 14:2-3] "In my Father's house are many mansions; if it were not so, I would have told you. I go to prepare a place for you. And if I go and prepare a place for you, I will come again, and receive you unto myself; that where I am there ye may be also." He who gave His life for our redemption, will come again to take us unto Himself.

The Power of God's Protection:

One of the enduring attributes of God is His power to protect His people, individually and collectively. In the second part of this message to Abram, God said "I am thy shield" This was not the promise of an army general or a police commissioner who was competent to offer protection that he could not deliver. These words came from the lips of the One who could protect from the most dangerous situations.

The Omnipotent, Omniscient, Omnipresent and Personal God, identified Himself as the protector of the man of faith who walked with Him, and with all who still walk by faith. The Psalmist confirmed this when he wrote [Psalm 46:1-4] "God is our refuge and strength a present help in trouble. Therefore will not we fear, though the earth be removed, and be carried into the midst of the sea; though the waters thereof roar and be troubled, though the mountains shake with the swelling thereof. There is a river, the streams whereof shall make glad the city of God, the holy place of the tabernacles of the Most High."

The Fullness of God's Reward:

In the third part of the message, the Lord said, "I am thy exceeding great reward." Abram was being rewarded for making a righteous decision. He refused the reward of the king of Sodom with its earthly value and obtained the reward of the King of glory. The great decision of

Christians is not to invest in earthly rewards that will make them rich in material things in this world, but to "lay up treasures in heaven." Christians should live by faith and then leave everything to God. Scripture says [Matthew 6:33] "Seek ye first the kingdom of God, and his righteousness; and all these things shall be added unto you."

Overwhelmed by the fullness of the blessings of God, David said [Psalm 103:1-5] "Bless the LORD, O my soul, and all that is within me, bless his holy name. Bless the LORD, O my soul, and forget not all his benefits. Who forgiveth all thine iniquities; who healeth all thy diseases; Who redeemeth thy life from destruction; Who crowneth thee with loving-kindness and tender mercies; Who satisfieth thy mouth with good things; so that thy youth is renewed like the eagles."

It is the LORD'S delight and desire to reconcile His people to Himself and to reward them. Both reconciliation and reward come through faith and absolute dependence on God. When He desired to be the "Covenant people's" reward, He invited them to a summit saying [Isaiah 1:18] "Come now, and let us reason together saith the LORD: though your sin be as scarlet, they shall be as white as snow; though they be red as crimson, they shall be as wool."

God did not only reward Abram with the land of Canaan,

but He declared Himself as Abram's reward. According to the teaching of the New Testament, the primary purpose of the Incarnation of Jesus Christ was that Christians should be rewarded with the full revelation of God. John wrote [1 John 5:20] "...We know that the Son of God is come, and hath given us an understanding, that we may know him that is true, and we are in him that is true, even in his Son Jesus Christ. This is the true God and eternal life."

The greatest reward that God can bestow on us is a fuller and better relationship with Himself. This is what Jesus promised when He said [John 14:16] "... I will pray the Father, and he shall give you another comforter, that he might abide with you for ever." God's promise to Abram was given to him after he had refused the worldly gifts of the king of Sodom [Gen. 14:23] "...I will not take from a thread even a shoelachet, and that I will not take any thing that is thine, lest thou shouldest say, I have made Abram rich." Every sacrificial choice and righteous decision that a Christian makes for the Lord Jesus Christ will bring exceeding great reward.

The Result of God's Promises:

Hans Kung wrote: "The Christian believes, not in the Bible, but in Him who it attests; the Christian believes, not in tradition, but in Him whom it transmits; the Christian believes not in the Church, but in Him who it proclaims."

Abram believed the LORD and accepted His promise, he acted decisively on the Word of God and it is recorded [Gen. 15:6] "...he believed in the LORD; and he counted it to him for righteousness."[2]

We can reflect on the fact that his reward was the result of righteousness, not of works but of faith in God. Paul confirmed this when he wrote to the Christians in Rome, saying [Rom. 4:3, 13] "Abraham believed God, and it was counted unto him for righteousness... For the promise that he should be the heir of the world, was not to Abraham, or his seed, through the law, but through the righteousness of faith..." This means that faith in God is the transforming power of life.

Under the Old Covenant Abram was justified by faith and for Christians Justification is still relevant by faith. God justifies the believer through Jesus Christ and grants them His peace. Paul, reassured the believers [Rom. 5:1-2] "Therefore being justified by faith, we have peace with God through our Lord Jesus Christ: by whom also we access by faith, and rejoice in the hope of the glory of God..." The Lord accepts faithful Christians as righteous. This faith in God and His Son Jesus Christ, embraces the yielded-ness of our whole selves to God, that He may be

2 Standing on the promises of Christ my King,
Through eternal ages let His praises ring;
Glory in the highest I will shout and sing,
Standing on the promises of God.

to us our exceeding great reward and that He work in us both to His will and good pleasure.

WALKING BEFORE GOD

And when Abram was ninety years old and nine, the LORD appeared to Abram, and said unto him, I [am] the Almighty God; walk before me, and be thou perfect. Gen. 17:1

The author George Ade said of a certain man, "He walks like he had a gravel in his shoes." Of a certain woman Balzac wrote, "She walked with a proud, defiant step, like a martyr to the coliseum." Of a woman also, Byron wrote, "She walks in beauty like the night of cloudless climes and starry skies. And Shakespeare wrote, "Walk the sprites to countenance this horror."

The Friendship:

Thirteen years had passed since the birth of Ishmael and "Abraham was ninety and nine years old and the Lord called unto him saying" [Gen. 17:1] "I am the Almighty God; walk before me, and be that perfect." The words 'Almighty God', was translated from the Hebrew word 'El Shadday'. El denotes 'power' and 'Shadday' was derived from the Akkadian Shadadu, which means to 'overpower'; portraying God as the overpowering, Almighty One who will supremely provide for Abraham.

Thus, he called to Abraham to walk in true fellowship

with Him. Age may have shut out companionship, joy and strength from Abraham, but he was not too old to have fellowship with the Almighty God. It was experience and faith that ripened his friendship with God. There is a chorus, which says, "I am a friend of God, He calls me friend."

How would you define the term 'friend'? A friend is a person with whom one has a close pleasant relationship. The historian says [Exodus 33:11] God spoke to Moses face to face as a man speaking unto his friend. Nevertheless, the only man who was called a friend of God was Abraham [James 2:23] "And the scripture was fulfilled which states, Abraham believed God, And it was imputed unto him for righteousness: and he was called a friend of God." The lesson Christians can learn from this is: A true friend will correct you enough because he or she wants you to arrive at your internal destination with all joy.

John Sammis, in his observation of those who walk with the Lord wrote:

> "When we walk with the Lord, In the light of his word, What a glory he sheds on our way! While we do his good will, He abides with us still, And with all who will trust and obey.
>
> Then in fellowship sweet We will sit at his feet, Or we'll walk by his side in the way; What he says we will do, Where

he sends we will go, Never fear, only trust and obey."[1]

The Identification:

The protection of identity has become a major problem in our digital and technological age; a person can steal your identity and cause you great distress and difficulty. They can take a photograph of your head and put it on a different body quite easily. They can take a photograph and place you among people you have never met and they can put you into positions and situations where you have never been.

Yes! Some people pay large sums of money each year to protect their identity and property. When a person's identity is stolen, their character and good name are also stolen. As Christians, we need to keep a Bible in our right hand and a newspaper in our left hand. In recent weeks, we have had some high-profile cases making news because of wrong identification.

When God identified Himself to Abraham, He said, "I am the Almighty God." This was Divine medication that was guaranteed to heal Abram's and every human person's sorrows; there is Divine forgiveness in that name to cleanse every sinner and remove every sin; there was Divine consolation to comfort every wounded heart; there was Divine resources to meet every human need. In

1 Church Hymnal, Northampton: New Testament Church of God, 1990, p136

those words are a Divine promise waiting to be fulfilled.

The LORD had promised Abram a son, but he was now getting old and no son was given to him. However, in the words of identification he had enough to brighten his faith and trim afresh the flickering lamp of hope. This identification of God as his all-sufficiency was revealed to him. For Christians this same all-sufficiency has been revealed in Jesus Christ.

The Resource:

There is more than enough in Jesus Christ to meet every human need, both for Christians and non-Christians. Paul told the Philippian Christians [Phil. 4:19] "My God shall supply all your needs according to his riches in glory by Christ Jesus." The weary, downcast pilgrim can listen to God's voice saying [Isa. 45:22] "Look unto me and be saved, all the ends of the earth: for I am God, and there is no else." He is the all-sufficient God.

The identity of our God cannot be stolen or be sold. He alone is Self-generating, Omnipotent, Omniscient, Omnipresent and Immutable. He said to Abram, "Walk before me." Those words were relevant for Abram and the Covenant people and they are relevant for the Redeemed people today.

To walk before God, means that He is forever watching over us. J. M. Hanson wrote:

All along on the road to the soul's true abode, There's an eye watching you; Every step that you take this great eye is awake; There's an eye watching to you.

As you make life's great fight, Keep the pathway of right. There's an eye watching you. God will warn not to go in the path of the foe, There's an eye watching to you.

Fix your mind on the goal, That sweet home of the soul, There's an eye watching you; Never turn from the way to the kingdom of day, There's an eye watching to you.[2]

The Almighty God of Abram and the Christians is a God of love, consolation and comfort, a God who fills the soul and hearts of His own.[3]

The Command:

"Walk before me, and be thou perfect." It may well be that Abram had been walking too much before Sarai, seeking to please her because she was a fair woman. He may well have been guided by her counsel, as he had already done. The record we have says [Gen. 16:1–4] "Now Sarah, Abram's wife, bare him no children: and she had an handmaid, and Egyptian, whose name was Hagar. And Sarai said unto Abram, Behold now, the LORD hath restrained me from bearing:

I pray thee, go in unto my maid; it may be that I may

2 Ibid p366
3 1 Sam. 15:22Acts 5:29

obtain children by her. And Abram hearkened to the voice of Sarai. And Sarai, Abram's wife, took Hagar her maid the Egyptian, after Abram had dwelt ten years in the land of Canaan, and gave her to her husband Abram to be his wife." In walking before Sarai and obeying her, he had turned from the life of faith in God. The creature had become more prominent in his life than the Creator.

The command "Walk before me, and be thou perfect" did two things for Abram:

1. It affected his life:

In all things and every day, his lifestyle was to be in the Directive will of the Almighty God. This was not to be a lifestyle of dread and awkward restraint, but a holy, joyful, sanctified and Divinely satisfied lifestyle. It is the life of faith and faithfulness. This was the high privilege of Abram and of every "Born-again" child of God.

2. It affected his character:

"Be thou perfect." This was a command to single mindedness or, wholeheartedness. The words of David are so appropriate here [Psalm 12:2] "They speak vanity everyone with his neighbour: with flattering lips and with a double heart do they speak." James added to this by saying [James 1:8] "A double minded man is unstable in all his ways." The Christians must make God their counsellor.

"Be perfect." All perfection comes from God, who alone is

perfect. The supreme human perfection lies in a single-mindedness and a wholehearted surrender before God. Each Christian should make a pledge of allegiance to serve God. In testifying of his allegiance, Dan Quayle said "I pledge allegiance to the Christian flag and to the Saviour, for whose kingdom it stands, One saviour, crucified, risen and coming again, with life and liberty for all who belief.[4]

The Submission:

In a prayer of submission, Thomas a Kempis said, "As thou wilt. What thou wilt: When thou wilt. Of it, Elizabeth Elliot wrote, "Supreme authority in both Church and home has been divinely vested in the male as representative of Christ, who is the Head of the Church. It is in willing submission rather than grudging capitulation that the woman in the church [whether married or single] and the wife in the home find their fulfilment.

After Abraham had received the command and promise [Gen. 16:3] "... He fell on his face: and God talked with him. His ears and heart were opened to hear and obey the voice of "The Almighty God." His actions demonstrated that he had a profound sense of his own ignorance and helplessness and these brought him to the right place to listen to God.

Repeatedly in scripture God spoke to the heart of the

4 Mark Water, The New Encyclopaedia of Christian Quotations, Hampshire: John Hunt Publications, 1995, p28

penitent; David had personal experience of this when he said [Psalm 34:18] "The Lord is nigh unto them that are of a broken heart; and saveth such as be of a contrite spirit." May the Almighty God who has commanded his people to "Walk before Him and be perfect." Grant us surrendered hearts and the spirit of peace that we may be sensitive to the promptings of the Holy Spirit.

The Transformation:

An unknown author wrote of the transforming power of God, "Nature forms us, sin deforms us, school informs us, Christ transforms us."[5] God did not only transform Abram's lifestyle but He also changed his name, He said to him [Gen. 17:5] "Neither shall thy name any more be called Abram, but thy name shell be Abraham; for a father of many nations have I made thee."

Complete surrender to God, brings complete transformation of character and nature. I am absolutely convinced that the man or woman, who walks in harmony and peace with God, walks in harmony and peace with his or her fellow creatures. Would you respond to the call of Jesus Christ today and walk before "The Almighty God?" Elisha A. Hoffman asked:

---

5 Ibid. p1062
Abram – High father, Abraham – Father of multitudes
Elisha A Hoffman, Church Hymnal, Northampton: New Testament Church of God, 1990, p425

You have longed for sweet peace, And for faith to increase, And have earnestly, fervently prayed, But you cannot have rest, or be perfectly blessed, until all on the altar is laid.

THE APPEARANCE OF THE LORD

And The Lord appeared unto him in the plains of Mamre: and he sat in the tent door in the heat of the day. Genesis 18:1

There are a variety of subjects enveloped in Abram's call to service. We have contemplated: The Discipline of Obedience [Genesis 12:1-2]; Absolute Commitment; Excellence In The Calling; Antecedent In The Calling; Understanding The Primacy Of The Call To Service; The Possession That God Promised Abram.

The Sojourn in Haran [Genesis 12:4]; we have looked at Worldly Wisdom and Divine Wisdom; The Purposeful Journey; The Moon Cult Of The Heathen Worshippers of Haran; The Entrance Into Canaan; The Inescapable Experiences; The Guaranteed Assurances Of God.

We have further looked at: the Sojourn in Egypt [Genesis 12:10]; The Testing of Faith; The Failure; The Fear; The Selfishness; The Hypocrisy; The Rebuke; The Recipient of The Rebuke; The Contagion; The Restoration. We have contemplated: Abram – The Man of Peace; The Impossible Relationship; Magnanimity The True Wealth; The Carnal Mind; The Spiritual Mind; and The Altar Of Testimony.

We have examined: The Reputation And Character Of

Abraham [Genesis 14:18-24]; Abram – The Man of Faith; Abram – The Man of Compassion; Abram – The Man of Courage; Abram – The Man of Unselfishness. We took time to ponder: The Words of Assurance [Genesis 15:1]; The Time of Assurance; The Message of Assurance; The Fullness of Assurance and The Result of Assurance.

Then we reflected on [Genesis 17:1]; The Command to Walk Before God; The Friendship of God; The Identification of God; The Resource of God; The Command of God; The Submission to God. These are only some of the subjects we have shared in recent months. Now let us go on to consider our theme for today:

The Appearance of the Lord:

"And the LORD appeared unto him in the plains of Mamre: and he sat in the tent door in the heat of the day. And he lifted up his eyes and looked, and three men stood by him: and when he saw them, he ran to meet them from the tent door, and bowed himself toward the ground.

It is without controversy that Christians can accept the way Old Testament events reveal some New Testament truths. Thus, we can reflect on this part of Abram's relationship to God, in this text and context [Genesis 18:1-17]. In the understanding of New Testament revelation, there is the clear revelation of Abraham, receiving and

1 Reputation is what we want people to know about us, but character is what God knows about us.

serving.

There are ten things that we can learn from this context:

The Accommodating Visit
The Generous Reception
The Longing Desire
The Eager Mind
This Submissive Spirit
The Willing Confession
Are Committed Fellowship
The Desire for Refreshment
The Readiness to Serve
The Blessed Reward

The Accommodating Visit:

The appearance of the LORD to Abraham is an amazing description of Divine Condescension and it is a typological mystery, that the Triune God would manifest Himself in the form of three Persons. This is an Incarnation that we have not seen before it is a revelation of the Trinity of the Eternal Godhead. The sovereign Trinity is committed to the saving of mankind and revealed in seeking to bless and to guide mankind in service.

The Father loved and sent "His only begotten Son"; the begotten Son loved and gave Himself up to death to redeem and reconcile mankind; the Holy Spirit loved and came to make His abode in the believing heart. This

Trinitarian belief or, threefold salvation is summed up in the New Testament Benediction [2 Cor. 13:14] "The grace of the Lord Jesus Christ, and the love of God, and the communion of the Holy Spirit."

The Gracious Reception:

The ministry of visitation can be demanding, challenging and welcoming. Christians today would do well with the domestic sanctuary of ancient times. In our modern sophisticated society, the ministry of visiting has to be arranged, classified, categorized and sanitized. This has created more problems for the church than we know. Instead of being Christianized, we have been Europeanized.

To visit some people appointments have to be made and visitors have to be selected; on the other hand, some Christian homes are closed to other Christians. This is unlike the fellowship that the Covenant People had and the Early Church practiced. The Bible says [Acts 2:46] "... they continuing daily with one accord in the temple, and in breaking bread from house to house, did eat their meat with gladness and singleness of heart."[2]

The way in which Abraham received the three visitors and his acts of generosity toward them, may serve to demonstrate how a thirsty and weary – longing soul may

---

2 Acts 2:42

welcome and accommodate Jesus Christ and become committed in serving Him.

The Longing to Desire:

The Shepherd of Hermas, made this request "Remove every evil desire and clothe yourself with good and holy desire. For if you are clothed with good desire, you will hate evil desire and bridle it as you please." The historian wrote of Abraham [Gen. 18:2] "... he lifted up his eyes and looked." The work of redemption has been established in the Christian man and woman, even before we lift up our eyes.

When David experienced: The Longing Desire for the things of God, he said [Psalm 121:1–2] "I will lift up my eyes unto the hills, from whence cometh with my help. My help cometh from the Lord, which made heaven and earth." The Lord is certain to appear in His sovereign grace to the waiting and watching Christians. According to the words of Jesus recorded in the gospel [Matt. 24:30] "... they shall see the Son of man coming in the clouds of heaven with power and great glory."

The writer of the Hebrew epistle said of the anticipation and desire for Christ's appearance [Heb. 9:28] "So Christ was once offered to bear the sins of many; and unto them that look for him shall he appear the second time without sin unto salvation.

In his epistle John said [1 John 3:2] "Beloved, now are we the sons of God, and it doth not yet appear what we shall be: but we know that, when he shall appear, we shall be like him; for we shall see him as he is." As Christians, we must continue to look up with a longing for Christ's appearance.[3]

The Eager Mind:

When Abraham saw the three visitors [Gen. 18:2] "He ran to meet them from the tent door." The man or woman who is living without affection, anticipation and expectation is content to stay where they are; they are not eager for greater things; they are satisfied with what they have and are; they live for the here and now.

But Christians like Abraham, have a promise and they are eager for its fulfilment. Sometimes the waiting seems long and wearisome, but we can be consoled by the words of the prophet [Isaiah 40:31] "... They that wait upon the LORD shall renew their strength; they shall mount up with wings as eagles; they shall run, and not to be weary, and they shall walk, and not faint." The Christians not only live in the here and now, but they anticipate the then and there.

Abraham met the three visitors with an eager and prepared mind. The Christians can be sure when their

---

3 John 3:1-10

souls are truly hungering for the living bread they will receive it with gladness. The Christians that are waiting for Jesus Christ will hasten to meet Him when he appears.

The Submissive Spirit:

The act of bowing toward the ground was a sign of humility. It demonstrated Abraham's submission to God. The nearer Christians come to Jesus Christ our Redeemer and Saviour, is the more unworthy we see ourselves to be and the more clearly we understand whose we are.

It must have been an occasion like this which prompted Fanny J. Crosby to write: "Consecrate me now to thy service Lord, By the power of grace divine; Let my soul look up with a steadfast hope, And my will be lost in Thine." The way to God is a self-humbling way; the nearer Christians come to His light the more unseeingly do the garments of our own righteousness appear.

The Willing Confession:

There is an old Scottish proverb that reads: "Confession is good for the soul."[4] This kind of confession is about a man or a woman having a right relationship with God, neighbours and themselves. Honest confession is linked to honest acknowledgement. Abraham's honest confession and honest acknowledgement came in two little words:

---

4   Robert Backhouse, 5000 Quotations, Eastbourne: Kingsway Publications, 1994, p39

[Gen. 18:3] "My Lord" and take note how the word Lord is written, it is "Adonai" a clear acknowledgement of Jesus Christ.

It is equal to the honest confession and honest acknowledgement of Simon Peter [Matt. 16:16] "Thou art the Christ, the Son of the living God." When Thomas made an honest confession and an honest acknowledgement in five words, he said [Luke 20:28] "My Lord and my God."

When a man or a woman comes into the real presence of Jesus Christ, we expect to hear them use the language of honest confession and honest acknowledgement. To say "My Lord" is to seal man's eternal destination. These two little words imply two great truths. 1. Appreciation and 2. Total Submission – God is mine and I am His.

The Commitment to Fellowship:

Abraham's commitment to fellowship is seen in the words to his visitors v.3 "Pass not away, I pray thee, from thy servant." Nothing was more important to Abraham than being in the presence of the Holy God. The man or woman who has found the presence of Jesus Christ will make every sacrifice to remain in it. To be in the presence of God is to enjoy the peace that passes all understanding and fullness of indescribable joy.

In our fellowship services we often sang:

What a fellowship, what a joy divine, Leaning on the

everlasting arms; What a blessedness, What a peace is mine, Leaning on the everlasting arms.

Jesus invites every sinner to find forgiveness and eternal hope in His love. Keep in mind – every Christian has a past and every sinner has a future.[5]

The Desire for Refreshment:

The plea to abide [v.4–5] "Let a little water, I pray you, be fetched, and wash your feet, and rest yourselves under the tree: And I will fetch a morsel of bread, and comfort ye your hearts; after that ye shall pass on: for therefore are ye come to your servant. And they said, So do, as thou hast said."

There are times when Christians are satisfied with getting God's blessings and favour, but stop short of seeking rest for His soul and comfort for His heart. Christ Jesus gave us rest and comfort by giving Himself for us: Let us give Him rest by giving ourselves to Him.

The Readiness to Serve:

In Abraham's action there was a readiness and a willingness to service, the Scripture says [Gen. 18:6–8] "Abraham hastened into the tent of Sarai, and said, make ready quickly three measures of fine meal, knead it, and make cakes upon the hearth. And Abraham ran unto the

_____
5 John 4

herd, and fetched a calf tender and good, and gave it unto a young man; and he hasted to dress it. And he took butter, and milk, and the calf which he had dressed, and set it before them; and he stood by them under the tree, and they did eat."

The lesson we have here is that true love for God gives freely; True love lends swiftness to willing feet. Since the early days of our faith, we have learnt that [2 Cor. 9:7] "The Lord loveth a cheerful giver." Paul told the Saints in Colossae [Col. 3:23] "Whatsoever ye do, do it heartily as unto the Lord." And to the saints at Corinth he said [2 Cor. 5:14–15] "... the love of Christ constraineth us; because we thus judge, that if one died for all, then were all dead: and that he died for all, that they which live should not henceforth live unto themselves, but unto him which died for them, and rose again."[6]

The Blessed Reward:

The three men, who represented the Holy Trinity, were on a Divine Mission when they visited Abraham. When they were about to depart, the Lord spoke, notice how the word Lord is written [v.17–18] "... The Lord said, Shall I hide from Abraham that thing which I do; seeing that Abraham shall surely become a great and mighty nation, and all the nations of the earth shall be blessed in him?"

---

6 Rev. 22:12

Reflecting on the pilgrimage of Abraham, the devil had tried everything to destroy him and his relationship with God, but he obeyed the command to walk before "The Almighty God and the perfect." He kept his eyes looking upward as he went forward. His devotion and commitment were rewarded with the revelation of the secret purpose of the Lord.

The secret of the Lord is with them that fear him. The entrance into the deep things of God are often revealed through self-sacrifice and active, ready and willing service. If you and I would know the hidden wisdom of God, and feed on the finest of the wheat, we must lay ourselves and all that we have at the feet of the Lord. We must open our hearts to Him and He will open His heart to us.

We are almost at the end of the Old Year and the beginning of the New Year, let us come together and renew our Covenant with God and with one another. Then let us join the words of the hymn writer and say:

> "I want to be a worker for the Lord, I want to love and trust His holy word, I want to sing and pray, and be busy every day, in the vineyard of the Lord.
>
> I will work, I will pray, In the vineyard, in the vineyard of the Lord. I will work, I will pray. I will labor every day, in the vineyard of the Lord.

I want to be a worker every day, I want to lead the erring in the way That leads to Heav'n above, Where all is peace and love, In the vineyard of the Lord.

I want to be a worker strong and brave, I want to trust in Jesus' pow'r to save; All who will truly come Shall find a happy home In the vineyard of the Lord.

I want to be a worker; help me, Lord, To lead the lost and erring to Thy Word, That points to joys on high Where pleasures never die, In the vineyard of the Lord.

THE ALL-DETERMINING QUESTION

Is anything too hard for the LORD? At the time appointed I will return unto thee, according to the time of life, and Sarah shall have a son. Gen. 18:14

We often sing a medley of choruses, which say:

> *"Only believe, only believe, all things are possible, only believe. Lord I believe, Lord I believe, all things are possible, Lord I believe. Lord I receive, Lord I receive, all things are possible Lord I receive. Help my unbelief, help my unbelief, all things are possible, help my unbelief."*

There are seven things that I would like to share with you from this text, they are:

The Sovereign Truth
The Promise
The Barrenness
The Provision
The Eavesdropping
The Denial
The Appointed Time

The Sovereign Truth:

Central to scripture is the sovereign truth that Man's impossibilities are God's possibilities. Whatever God has created, he has created with the ability to produce and reproduce; God has never changed, reversed or suspended this design. The earliest historical evidence of this revelation says [Gen. 27-28] "... God created man in his own image, in the image of God created he him; male and female created he them.[1]

And God blessed them and God said unto them, be fruitful, and multiply, and replenish the earth, and subdue it: and have dominion over the fish of the sea, and over the fowl of the air, and over every living thing that moveth upon the earth."

The Promise:

Before the sovereign God makes promise to any man or woman, He made provision for its fulfilment. Aeschylus wrote, "God's lips know not how to lie, but He will accomplish all His promises."[2] The apostle Paul exhorted the saints in Corinth [2 Cor. 1:20] "... For all the promises of God in him are yeah, and in him amen, unto the glory of God by us.

---

1 Man has not to explain creation, but to receive it. The God of creation is also the God of arrangements. The Creator of the sun is also the creator of the Grass! What a condescension!

Gen. 18:22; 19:1; Rom. 1:24–27; Jude 7
2 Mark Water, The New Encyclopaedia of Christian Quotations, Hampshire: John Hunt Publications, 1995, p834

2 Cor. 1:20; Heb. 11:11

In the nature of reproduction, God has created the male with the seed and the female with the womb to fulfil His Divine purpose. In the primacy of His promise to Abram, God said [Gen. 12:2] "... I will make of thee a great nation and I will bless thee, and make thy name great; and thou shalt be a blessing.

According to scripture, whenever God changes a person's name a blessing is on its way [Gen. 17:15–16] "God said unto Abraham, as for Sarai thy wife, thou shalt not call her name Sarai, but Sarah shall be her name. And I will bless her, and give thee a son also of her, and she shall be a mother of nations; kings of people shall be of her.

The Barrenness:

It was Sarah's barrenness and desperation that have caused her to give Abraham her handmaid [Gen. 16:1–2] "Now Sarah, Abram's wife, bare him no children: and she had a handmaid, an Egyptian, whose name was Hagar. And Sarah said unto Abram, Behold now, the Lord hath restrained me from bearing: I pray thee, go in unto my maid; it may be that I may obtain children by her. And Abram hearkened unto the voice of Sarah.

What Sarah did was according to the legal custom as seen in the legal codes of that time, but it was in opposition to the plan of and timing of God. Thus, God called to Abram and said [Gen. 17:1] "I am the Almighty God walk before me and be thou perfect." In other words, God said: Sarah did not command you to leave Ur of the Chaldea; Sarah did not make the promise to give you a son; Sarah did not promise to bless you and make you a great nation."

The Provision:

In the nature of reproduction, there was a special seed and there was a special womb in the plan of God. His future purpose had already been fixed, concerning the twelve tribal leaders for Israel. Prior to the conception of Isaac, God had a predestined plan of a ram to be caught in a thicket on mount Moriah.

That part of God's plan was not yet revealed to Abraham because Isaac had not yet been conceived; he was still waiting on the fulfilment of the promise. The Scripture says [Gen. 22:13] "Abraham lifted up his eyes, and looked, and behold behind him a Ram caught in a thicket by his horns: and Abraham went and took the ramp, and offered him up for a burnt offering in the stead of his son. And Abraham called the name of the place Jehovah-Jireh: as it is said to this day; in the mount of the Lord it shall be see." All of this could not have come to pass without God's miraculous intervention.

The Eavesdropping:

Eavesdropping is listening in on other people's conversation and it can have serious consequences. The visitors asked [Gen. 18:9–12] "Where is Sarah thy wife? And he said, Behold in the tent. And he said, I will certainly return unto thee according to the time of life; and lo, Sarah thy wife shall have a son. And Sarah heard it in the tent door, which was behind him.

Now Abraham and Sarah were old and well stricken in age: and it ceased to be with Sarah after the manner of women. Therefore Sarah laughed within herself, saying: after I am waxed old shall I have pleasure, my lord being also old? The Denial:

Sarah saw the impossibility of Abraham and herself ever having a child in their "Old and well stricken age." The law of nature said it was impossible; Sarah's biology said it was impossible; Abraham's biology said it was impossible, but God's promise said it was possible and the plan for it was agreed and sealed in eternity past.

Doubting laughter cannot alter the promise of God; time cannot abandon the promise of God; denial cannot alter the promise of God. All of these things have been tried and failed and now God asked [Gen. 18:14] "Is anything too hard for the Lord?" This is The All-determining Question of the ages. Abraham had to answer it; Sarah had to answer it and you and I have to answer it.

The Appointed Time:

One of the three visitors said [v.14] "At the appointed time I will return unto thee according to the time of life, and Sarah shall have a son." God had a special seed and a special womb through which He planned the coming of the twelve tribal leaders of Israel; And he had a special seed and a special womb through which He planned the birth of Jesus Christ and the calling of the twelve apostles of the Church.

God planned the event on mount Moriah and He planned the event on mount Calvary. When Sarah heard the plan of God in her old age she laughed and when Mary heard it in her young age she said [Luke 2:46] "My soul doth magnify the Lord, and my spirit hath rejoiced in God my Saviour." The nature of the law of conception was fixed, but the Lawgiver is greater than the law. Thus the question was asked "Is anything too hard for the Lord?"

Our reaction can be summed up in the reassuring hymn of six verses by William Cowper:

> *God moves in a mysterious way His wonders to perform; He plants His footsteps in the sea And rides upon the storm.*

> *Deep in unfathomable mines Of never failing skill He treasures up His bright designs And works His sovereign will.*

> *Ye fearful saints, fresh courage take; The clouds ye so much dread Are big with mercy and shall break In blessings on your head.*

> *Judge not the Lord by feeble sense, But trust Him for His*

grace; Behind a frowning providence, He hides a smiling face.

His purposes will ripen fast, Unfolding every hour; The bud may have a bitter taste, But sweet will be the flower.

Blind unbelief is sure to err And scan His work in vain; God is His own interpreter, And He will make it plain.